The
Smokeless Coal Fields
of
West Virginia

Tams, WV, showing the tipple, offices, and company store, c. 1920. (From the George Bragg collection.)

The
Smokeless Coal Fields
of
West Virginia

A Brief History

W. P. Tams, Jr.

Second Edition
Introduction by Ronald D Eller

West Virginia University Press
Morgantown
2001

West Virginia University Press, Morgantown 26506
© 1963, 1983, 2001 by West Virginia University Press
All rights reserved
First edition published 1963. Second edition 2001
Printed in the United States of America

10 09 08   5 4 3 2

ISBN 0-937058-55-6

Library of Congress Cataloging-in-Publication Data

Tams, W[illiam] P[urviance], Jr. 1883-1977
   The smokeless coal fields of West Virginia; a brief history / W .
   P . Tams, Jr.—2nd ed. with an introduction by Ronald D
   Eller.
   114 p. maps 23 cm.
1. Coal mines and mining — West Virginia — History.
2. Coal miners — West Virginia. 3. West Virginia — History. I.
Title.
HD9547.W4 2001   2001088424
                                                 LCCN

Cover Photograph courtesy of West Virginia & Regional History
      Collection
Photographs of Tams, WV, courtesy of George Bragg Collection
Book design by Sara Pritchard
Printed in USA by Chas. M. Henry Printing Company

Contents

Introduction (by Ronald D Eller) 1

Preface 11

Introduction 12

Location and Early Development........................15

Finances and Organization 24

Work in the Mines at the Turn of the Century 34

The Gulf Smokeless Coal Company 51

Personalities in the Smokeless Coal Fields...........74

Place Names in the Smokeless Coal Fields.......100

Statistical Table..107

The town of Tams, with miners' houses and the Baptist and Catholic churches. c. 1920. (From the George Bragg collection.)

Introduction

by **Ronald D Eller**

On a cold March morning in 1975 I pulled into the little town of Tams, West Virginia. Tams resembled scores of other declining mining towns in Appalachia. Double rows of gray company houses squatted in the narrow valley beneath a steep hillside to my right, while a rusting coal tipple sat astride empty railroad tracks farther up the hollow. I parked in front of a well-kept bungalow in the center of the village across from the old company store. This was not the kind of residence that one expected for a coal baron, but William Purviance Tams, Jr. was no typical coal baron. Tams had come to West Virginia in 1904 at the height of the great coal boom and had remained long after most of his contemporaries had made their fortunes and left. Now almost 100 years old and slowed by a recent stroke, Tams was the last of a generation of pioneer coal operators that had transformed the mountains into one of the worlds richest coal fields —and Appalachia into one of the nation's poorest regions.

A nurse greeted me at the door and ushered me into a small study lined with bookcases and cluttered with newspapers and old files. Beyond the study was an even more dimly lit sitting room and in an overstuffed chair sat Major Tams, his lap covered by a throw and his eyes fixed on the tipple that lay beyond the plate glass window. In the corner near his chair was a stack of *Playboy* magazines containing a current article about his life. In recent years Tams had become something of a celebrity and, despite his weakened condition, he relished the opportunity to share his story with visitors. Unlike most of his contemporaries, Tams had outlived an important historical era and was eager to share his unique perspective on the past. Frail and weakened by his stroke, the Major took charge of the interview. He was still in command of his world.

Although Tams did not remember the family, my grandfather had worked in the Tams mine during the 1920s and my father was born in the neighboring coal camp of Helen. When my grandfather learned that I intended to interview Tams for a book I was writing on the history of Appalachia, he asked why I wanted to interview "that old man." The town of Tams was a nice place to live, he explained. It had electric lights in every home, the first bathhouse for miners, and the first movie house in the area. But the Major "ran a tight ship" and if you lived there you had to "toe the line." Indeed, where many early coal operators gradually sold their holdings and moved away or left their operations under the control of mine managers, Tams continued to reside in the community throughout his life, even after he sold the company in 1955. A bachelor whose entire world revolved around his work, he ran the mine and the town with a personal concern that went beyond the production of coal itself. After all, Tams noted, this was "his community," and he "wanted a decent place to live." [1] Along with many businessmen at the turn of the century, he epitomized Alexis de Tocqueville's "ambitious men in democracies ... [who] care much more for success than for fame. What they most ask of men is obedience, what they most covet is empire." [2]

---

[1] William Purviance Tams, Jr., interview by Ronald D Eller, transcript, March 8, 1975, Southern Oral History Collection, University of North Carolina at Chapel Hill, 8.

[2] Alexis de Tocqueville, *Democracy in America* (New York: Harper & Row, 1966), 607.

William P. Tams also loved history, and when Robert F. Munn of the West Virginia University Library asked him in the early 1960s to compile a history of coal mining in southern West Virginia, Tams gladly complied. *The Smokeless Coal Fields of West Virginia* (1963), reprinted here, is much more, however, than a brief history of one of West Virginia's most productive coal regions. Written by a pioneer operator who served in leadership positions in the Winding Gulf Coal Operators Association, the Smoke-less Operators Association, the National Coal Association and the Southern Coal Operators Association, this little book constitutes a memoir of a man and a generation that shaped our history. Along with many other businessmen of that era, early coal operators generally shunned publicity, and they left few records and manuscripts from which to tell their story and explain their actions. Tams's description of the events, companies, and personalities that built the coal industry in the New River and Winding Gulf regions fills an important gap in our understanding of that volatile time.

The decades surrounding the turn of the twentieth century were years of dramatic transition in West Virginia and in much of Appalachia. Caught in the maelstrom of the industrial revolution that was sweeping the rest of the country, the region was tossed by rapid population growth, community building, and sudden political and economic change. Within a few short decades, central Appalachia was transformed from a land of scattered woodland farms into a bustling center of mines, saw mills and company towns. Families who had resided in the region for generations abandoned their traditional lifestyles and migrated to the new industrial communities where they were joined by African-American recruits from the deep South and southern European immigrants fresh from Ellis Island in New York. Like other Americans of that period, mountain families left their rural communities with great hope for the new world of industrial work, but in the coal fields they found opportunities limited by a pattern of modernization that drained away the new wealth and left only disappointment and poverty in its wake.

Railroads had begun to penetrate the mountains in the years following the Civil War in order to tap the rich reserves of coal, timber and other resources demanded by an industrializing nation. Along with the railroads came a gaggle of mineral buyers who bought millions of acres of mountain land for absentee land companies and later a flood of aspiring entrepreneurs intent upon making their fortune by developing the region's natural resources. Some of these entrepreneurs were natives of the mountains who sought to take advantage of the boom times, but most were outland capitalists. Many, like Tams, were well-educated descendents of established southern families. Others had worked as managers or mining engineers in the older Pennsylvania coal fields farther north. All shared a tenacity for success and a common business philosophy characteristic of their time. During an era of rapid social change, they were the "power elite" who shaped the course of development and influenced public policy in the coal communities and across the state. [3]

Coal barons differed as much from each other as did the company towns they built along the creeks and rivers

---

[3] See Ronald D Eller, *Miners, Millhands and Mountaineers: Industrialization of the Appalachian South, 1880 – 1930* (Knoxville: University of Tennessee Press, 1982); John Alexander Williams, *West Virginia and the Captains of Industry* (Morgantown: West Virginia University Press, 1976); Ronald L. Lewis, *Transforming the Appalachian Countryside: Railroads, Deforestation and Social Change in West Virginia, 1880 – 1920* (Chapel Hill: University of North Carolina Press, 1998); and John Hennen, *The Americanization of West Virginia: Creating a Modern Industrial State, 1916 – 1925* (Lexington: University of Kentucky Press 1996).

of southern West Virginia. Some took particular pride in maintaining modern living and working conditions. Others, less paternalistic, gave little thought to labor management or community responsibility. The latter applied something of an "ethics of the jungle" to their relationships with miners and usually took a more callous position on wages, mine safety, public health, taxation, and other social issues. Life was a competition for survival of the fittest, they reasoned, and the successful had no responsibility to the poor. Labor was a commodity that the miner had the right to sell and the operator had the right to buy under whatever conditions the market offered. Such attitudes fueled labor resistance and contributed to the popular image of the coal barons as the symbol of all that was evil in early industrial capitalism.

William Tams, Jr. had little respect for those operators who did not take an interest in providing good houses, sanitation, safe working conditions, good schools, and proper amusements for miners and their families. While he shared their self-interest in maximizing profits, Tams believed that the rich and successful had a responsibility to protect the poor and less fortunate and to create an environment that encouraged order, peace, and stability. Tams's old South paternalism (and his desire to prevent unionization) led him to pay higher wages than many operators in the Smokeless coal fields, to maintain a clean community, and to provide amenities that were rare in the region as a whole.

Yet even Tams's paternalism could not overcome basic assumptions about power that he shared with other coal operators. They all embraced a view of society that delegated power and authority to those who had demonstrated ability through material success. They all valued order and stability, discipline and obedience, and they all had a passionate dislike for labor unions. In order to assure the harmony and order of the coal camps and to protect their little kingdoms from outside interference, the coal barons employed their own private police force and early established control of local political systems. Almost every county government in the coal fields came under the control of the coal operators, and they used their power over Republican and Democratic candidates alike to limit taxation, control regulation, and otherwise protect their economic interests. Convinced that the miners' interests were identical to those of the company, they ruled the towns as they ruled the mines, without opposition or debate. In southern West Virginia where company towns outnumbered independently incorporated towns more than five to one, the new industrial order brought "company discipline" and the arbiter of effective jurisprudence was the coal baron. "To use the expression of the Middle Ages," Tams recalled, " I was the high justice, the middle and the low." [4]

In the pages that follow, Tams describes the arrival of the coal men and the world they created at the turn of the century. He traces the opening of the region by the Chesapeake and Ohio, the Norfolk and Western, and the Virginian railroads, and he sketches the financial structures that linked mine operators to the land companies, railroads, and to each other. He describes the challenges faced by pioneer operators who quickly found themselves in "peonage" to heavy royalties, differential railroad rates, and price fixing by railroad marketing agencies. This condition, he suggests, eventually led to the consolidation of smaller mines and the creation of independent marketing agencies and coal operators associations. Illustrating

---

[4] Laurence Leamer, "Twilight For a Baron: Major William Purviance Tams, Jr.," *Playboy*, May 1973, 168.

these structures, Tams delineates the history of his own company, the Gulf Smokeless Coal Company, and of a major West Virginia land-holding company, the Beaver Coal Company.

Such early competitive pressures, he argues, influenced the evolution of life in the coal fields at the turn of the century. Having acquired a lease to mine coal, the pioneer operator had to recruit laborers quickly in order to begin production and recuperate some return on his investment. "The operators built towns because they had no alternative," Tams attests. Since most mines were opened in virtually unsettled areas, houses had to be built for miners, and "the operators were the only ones with the capital and the organization to do the job." Similarly, company stores and the infamous scrip system evolved to meet the needs of miners in a remote region. The profits made by the company stores varied widely, he admits. "Some companies took advantage of a near monopoly and charged all the traffic would bear," but others, including those controlled by Tams, "operated on a profit margin considerably below that general among private stores in the area."

Scrip was one of many "conveniences" extended to the miner and his family by the mine operator. This form of credit was available to all employees, Tams points out, and —at least in his area —miners were not required to ask for scrip. Some "men who were careless in money matters" abused the system, and "it was a cheap and easy trick for union organizers or for competing and envious merchants to brand the company store as a robber." But, Tams believes, company stores deserved "only a fraction of the abuse" traditionally hurled against them. "Salaried employees were usually given their store goods at cost," and the average miner could choose to pay in cash if he desired. Tams adds that many coal companies also built churches and school buildings at each mining camp and supplemented the school year provided by the county with an additional two months of school. Medical fees were deducted from each miner's pay and a company doctor was available for every two or three mines. In contrast to the view of the company town by many critics of the coal industry who believed that this system was "imposed on helpless miners by rapacious operators," Tams draws a different, more congenial portrait of the coal community.

The world that the coal barons built was one of hard work and hard living. Tams describes the working day of a miner and his "buddy" during the hand-loading era at the turn of the century. He delineates the mining process where men first undercut, then blasted, and loaded coal into wooden cars to be hauled to the mine mouth by ponies or mules. Miners were paid only for the coal that they loaded, and they had to lay their own track to the coal face, set their own roof props, and clean their work site of debris before starting the process again. Mechanization gradually increased production, but it came with its own dangers of electrocution, explosions, and increased levels of coal dust. Tams provides a first hand description of two mine disasters in southern West Virginia and applauds the efforts by state and federal authorities to reduce explosions, but he laments that coal mining remained a hazardous occupation.

The difficulties and dangers of the mines contributed to the "wide-open" environment of drinking, gambling, and prostitution that prevailed around many of the mining camps in the area. Miners and operators alike in Fayette County frequented the saloons and gambling parlors along the New River, while baseball became a passion in other districts with some companies forming their own professional teams. Violence and the loss of work from over indulgence in these activities led operators to hire their own police. Crack shots such as Baldwin-Felts agents who were "deputized by the county sheriff but paid by the coal operators." Early miners "were a hard-bitten lot," observes Tams, and the employment of company-paid deputies—outlawed by the state legislature in 1935—was necessary to "preserve some semblance of order in the camps."

The practice of hiring private police fueled the intensity of labor violence in the coal fields, but Tams writes little about the "mine wars" that swept southern West Virginia in the first decades of the century. He attributes labor unrest to efforts by the northern operators in the Central Competitive Field to pressure the United Mine Workers to organize the southern coal fields. These efforts failed, he suggests, because southern West Virginia operators paid higher wages than the union scale, and it was not until the 1930's with the support of President Franklin Roosevelt that John L. Lewis was able to organize the area. Surprisingly, Tams is relatively uncritical of Lewis, whom he believed had administered the union welfare fund "honestly and economically." He also praises the UMW-sponsored miners' hospitals constructed throughout the region in the 1950s for providing quality care for miners and their families.

Tams's highest flattery, however, is reserved for the early operators who pioneered the development of the Smokeless coal fields. Unlike their modern counterparts who are the representatives of distant corporations, pioneer operators were a "highly individualistic lot" who raised the capital, selected the site, supervised the building of the town, and managed all aspects of the operation. No "remote figure," most lived in their communities and "took pride in knowing each of his employees." For this reason, Tams concludes, "the gulf between operators and miners was relatively small in the early days." In one of the most valuable portions of the book, Tams sketches brief biographies of more than two-dozen of these operators. The list of family names—including Berwind, Caperton, Dixon, Francis, Jones, Laing, Mann, and Tierney—reads like a Who's Who of political and economic power in southern West Virginia in the twentieth century.

These and other coal men shaped the history of the region at a time of great change. The private empires that they created left a deep mark on several generations of mountain families. Ironically, Tams believes that it was not the coming of the union, the vagaries of the market, or the rise of government regulation that brought an end to the reign of King Coal. The arrival of the automobile and good roads in the 1930s made it possible for the miners to live some miles from the mine and to retreat to growing towns like Beckley and Bluefield for entertainment and consumer goods. Gradually the company mining towns began to decline and with them the direct power of the coal barons over the lives of working families. By the 1960s the shabby ruins of hundreds of mining towns dotted the landscape in central Appalachia providing mute testimony to a lost era. The legacy of this time and the continuing influence of the industry that dominated it would survive into the next century. William Tams's brief history of the Smokeless Coal Fields provides a revealing window into this world that the coal barons made.

Ronald D Eller
Lexington, Kentucky
February 16, 2001

The
Smokeless Coal Fields
of
West Virginia

A Brief History

Preface

This brief and somewhat fragmentary history of coal mining in Southern West Virginia has been compiled at the request of Dr. Robert F. Munn, Director of Libraries, West Virginia University. Dr. Munn has given a great deal of help on the work by suggestions, editing, and the furnishing of some information not in my possession.

Among the many weaknesses of the work is the lack of information as to the Kanawha and Williamson coal fields due to my having had no direct contact with those areas.

Also, I wish to remind any who read this effort that it is based on personal recollections reaching back more than half a century and may well contain errors, especially as to personalities, for which I apologize herewith.

The men who pioneered the coal fields had virtues as imperishable as the rock that overlies the coal seams, and faults that have disappeared like the impurities that are cleaned out of the coal. I hope the same can be said of this work.

W. P. Tams, Jr.

Introduction

In any law court, before a witness can be accepted as an "expert", he must qualify as such by stating his training and experience. For that reason, it might be well for the writer to give a brief account of himself.

I was born in Staunton, Virginia in 1883. I attended the public school there and then entered Virginia Polytechnic Institute, where I graduated, summa cum laude, in 1902. After a year's graduate work as an instructor, I worked in the construction engineer's office of the Seaboard Air Line Railway on the Atlanta to Birmingham branch. I then got a position with the E. I. du Pont de Nemours Company in Wilmington, Delaware.

At that time my uncle, Mr. Harry Frazier, a consulting engineer who had been Chief Engineer of the Chesapeake and Ohio Railway Company, was supervising the building of a branch railway for Mr. Samuel Dixon, a major coal operator in Fayette County, West Virginia. In answer to an inquiry by Mr. Dixon for a young engineer, my uncle suggested my name, and Mr. Dixon employed me. I came to West Virginia on October 1, 1904 and served four years as an engineer for Mr. Dixon.

In 1908, with my friend and associate, James O. Watts of Lynchburg, Virginia, I secured a lease of coal property on the Winding Gulf in Raleigh County. With the help of my former employer, Mr. Dixon, I opened the Tams mine of the Gulf Smokeless Coal Company and commenced shipment October 1, 1909. I was successively vice president and general manager, and president of the company. I was a charter member of the Winding Gulf Operators Association, member and president in 1928 of the Smokeless Operators Association, member of the National Coal Association, member and director of the Southern Coal Operators Association, and member of the Board of Directors of District No. 7, under the Guffey Bill. During all of that time, until I sold out in 1955, I acted for my company as operating manager, chief engineer, and handled all sales. All told, I have had rather broad experience in the Smokeless Coal Field of West Virginia.

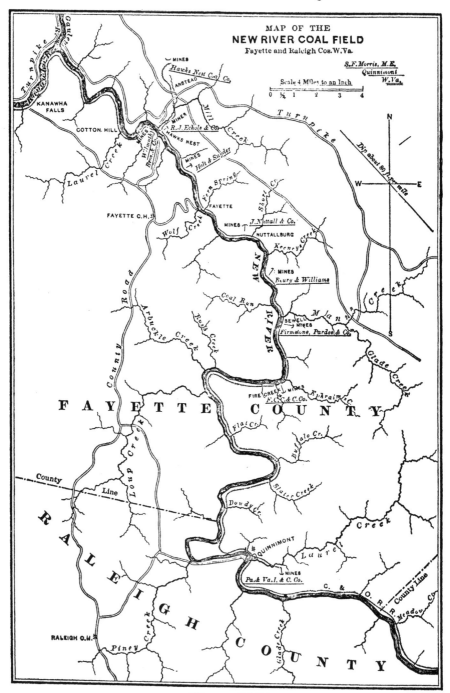

MAP OF THE
NEW RIVER COAL FIELD
Fayette and Raleigh Cos. W. Va.

S. F. Morris, M. E.
Quinnimont
W. Va.

Scale 4 Miles to an Inch

Circa 1879

1

Location and Early Development

The coal-producing areas of the New River Valley, the Kanawha Valley and that part of West Virginia lying south of those two rivers are called "The Southern West Virginia Coal Fields." The western portion comprises the Kanawha, The Guyandotte, and the Williamson fields, from north to south. The eastern portion comprises the New River, the Winding Gulf, and the Pocahontas fields, also from north to south.

The Kanawha, Guyandotte, and Williamson fields contain high volatile coals, and the New River, Winding Gulf, and Pocahontas fields produce low volatile, or "smokeless" coals. The more volatile matter, or gas, which a coal contains the more smoke it makes when being burned. The high volatile coals contain from 32 to 38 percent volatile matter. The low volatile coals contain from 16 to 24 percent volatile matter, and hence are called "smokeless." All coal was originally burned by hand firing, and the smoke difference between the high and low volatile coals was considerable. Anthracite coal has only 6 to 8 percent volatile matter, hence its early popularity in large cities where smoke was a great consideration. When John Mitchell called the great anthracite strike in 1902, the low volatile coals of West Virginia furnished the nearest approach to anthracite and built up a reputation and a market that stood them in good stead later on.

Early History

After the Revolution, the State of Virginia took over sovereignty of former Crown lands. The debts owed by the State to officers who had served in the War were discharged by offering in payment lands in the western part of the State at 10 cents per acre. Many officers sold their warrants at a discount to speculators, and sizable patents were thus accumulated. For example, the Moore and Beckley patent covered 175,000 acres, the James Welch patent 90,000 acres, and the Wilson Cary Nicholas patent 500,000 acres. To be issued a deed, it was required that the patentee survey and map the tract and file the map with the Land Office in Richmond. Most of the area covered by these patents was non-arable land, but underlaid with coal. The occurrence of coal had been noted in the middle of the 18th century by the exploring parties of Dr. Thomas Walker of Albemarle County and of Andrew Lewis of Greenbrier County. After the Civil War, the owners of these patents were, as a rule, unable to meet the taxes levied by West Virginia and forfeited the lands to the State. The State then put the forfeited lands up for sale to help finance the new public schools. Investors, chiefly from Pennsylvania, who had experience in the coal industry and were aware of the profit to be made from coal, bought up these lands. They were then prepared to lease them to coal operators, whenever such lands were reached by railways.

Entry of the Railroads

Three major railroads serve the smokeless coal fields: The Chesapeake and Ohio, the Norfolk and Western and the Virginian. A more-or-less distinct field grew up along the lines of each. In the following sections I have attempted to outline the early development of these fields.

The Chesapeake and Ohio

Well before the Civil War, the State of Virginia, realizing the need for transportation to the western portion of the State, built five main roads across the Allegheny Mountains. These were constructed under the supervision of Col. Claude Crozet, a French army engineer who had been with Napoleon in the Russian campaign and who had fled France after Waterloo. Virginia also started the James River and Kanawha Canal, which was completed up the James River to Buchanan and from Charleston up the Kanawha to Deepwater. The plans of this canal included a four-mile tunnel through the mountains—a major undertaking. However, the railway era dawned and canals were soon all but forgotten.

The State of Virginia started in the 1840's the Virginia Central Railroad (now the C. & O.) from Richmond in the east and from Charleston in the west. When the Civil War started the road was in operation from Richmond to Clifton Forge, and considerable work had been done on the western end. In fact, during the first year of the war, work continued on the Second Creek tunnel, near Ronceverte.

After the Civil War, C. P. Huntington, who was one of the builders of the Central Pacific

Railway, acquired the Virginia Central from the Virginia Legislature, and proceeded to complete the railway through the mountains and down New River and the Kanawha to Charleston, and thence to Huntington. This opened the New River and Kanawha coal fields by at last furnishing transportation to coal markets in 1872-3. Coal mines were soon opened on the main line of the railway. Branch lines were then built to reach other coal land and mines were opened on these branches.

In 1893 the Chesapeake and Ohio Railway built a branch line up Loop Creek from Thurmond to Kilsyth, and mines were opened in the thick (5 foot to 8 foot) Sewell seams, by John McGuffin, Justus Collins, James Laing, Samuel Dixon and by the land owner, T. G. McKell. Similar developments were made along the Kanawha River in the high volatile fields, and on branch railway lines in both the New River and Kanawha fields.

The Norfolk and Western

The beginnings of the Norfolk and Western Railway can be traced back to 1837, when a few miles of railroad were constructed between Petersburg and the James River. By the time the Civil War started, a line connecting Norfolk and Bristol, Tennessee had been constructed. However, the present-day Norfolk and Western came into being with the purchase in 1881 of the Atlantic, Mississippi and Ohio Railroad by the powerful Philadelphia banking firm of E. W. Clark and Company.

The management of the newly-named Norfolk and Western was well aware of the potential value of the Flat Top region and was determined to reach it. Surveys were made and the necessary franchises obtained as quickly as possible, and actual construction of seventy-five miles of narrow gauge track was begun in August 1881. In March 1883, after an expenditure of almost $2,000,000, the rails reached Pocahontas. The first shipment of Pocahontas coal was made the same month. At first, coal was transferred at Radford to standard gauge cars. When the mine proved successful, the narrow gauge was widened to standard gauge. By 1893, the line had been extended west to Kenova, West Virginia, opening up the Pocahontas and the Williamson fields.

The Pocahontas Mine was the first opened on this railway. The Pocahontas No. 3 seam was 12 feet thick at this point, and continued as a thick seam for miles westward. It was the seam offering the lowest cost of coal mining in Southern West Virginia. Shortly after the Civil War, this area had been prospected by Major Jed Hotchkiss, who had been a topographical engineer on Stonewall Jackson's staff and who was an all-round scientist. Major Hotchkiss published a magazine, THE VIRGINIAS, promoting the possibilities of the West Virginia and Southwest Virginia coal fields and lectured on this subject in Philadelphia, New York and New England. His efforts resulted in the opening of the Pocahontas mine and the Pocahontas field generally. He interested J. C. Maben of Philadelphia in purchasing the James Welch patent of 90,000 acres on the head waters of the Guyandotte River and

had a half interest with Maben in this tract. Today no memorial of this pioneer scientist of the
coal fields remains, except an insignificant station on the Virginian Railway.

As the Pocahontas field developed, mining
men, chiefly from Pennsylvania, opened up mines.
The Norfolk and Western Railway, through a
subsidiary company, had acquired ownership of
the old Wilson Cary Nicholas patent, reduced to
375,000 acres, and leases were made by the land
company to various pioneers such as the Tierney
brothers, Ned Houston, W. H. McQuail, and others. These leases averaged 1,000 acres, and the
lessee was required to build one bee-hive coke
oven for each ten acres of lease. This was to provide a means of disposing of the slack coal in the
form of coke. As with the Chesapeake and Ohio
Railway, branch lines were built from time to
time and mines opened thereon.

The Virginian

Capt. William N. Page, a mining engineer and
a cousin of the author Thomas Nelson Page, in-
terested Mr. Henry H. Rogers, an associate of
John D. Rockefeller, in a 17,000 acre tract of coal
land near the Chesapeake and Ohio Railway at
Deepwater, about thirty miles east of Charleston.
To develop the property, it was necessary to build
several miles of railway from Deepwater up to
Page, the location of the mine. About 1903, Capt.
Page suggested that Rogers build a railway from
Page on to Matoaka. This would connect the Chesa-
peake and Ohio Railway at Deepwater and the
Norfolk and Western Railway at Matoaka, thus

opening up the country between the two main line railways. The Pennsylvania Railroad, feeling the competition of West Virginia coal in the eastern markets, had by 1901 purchased a controlling interest in both the Chesapeake and Ohio and the Norfolk and Western. (The Pennsylvania Railway later relinquished control of the Chesapeake and Ohio, but still retains control of the Norfolk and Western). Not wishing to see more coal mines opened, both the Chesapeake and Ohio and the Norfolk and Western resisted the effort of Mr. Rogers to build his connecting railroad.

When Page persuaded Rogers to build the railway from Deepwater to Matoaka, an investment of only $5,000,000 was contemplated. Mr. Rogers' name was kept out of it, and each month money for the contractors was furnished to the dummy officials of the Deepwater Railway. The construction was attributed to various sources, including the Wabash Railway, the Western Maryland Railway, Standard Oil and others.

When the C. & O. and the N. & W. definitely refused to give the Deepwater Railway a pro-rate on the coal to be hauled, Mr. Rogers became very angry. He decided to extend his road to Tidewater and later to extend it west to the Great Lakes, thus furnishing operators on his road access to all available markets. To prevent further obstruction by the two existing railways, this decision was kept secret. Louis R. Taylor, one of the Deepwater Railway engineers, was sent to make a reconnaissance survey of possible routes east through Virginia, riding horseback and posing as a tobacco buyer. When he had completed his mission, a consulting engineer in Philadelphia, C. P. Perrin, was employed to organize parties of locating engineers. With all necessary survey equipment, they were loaded on a southbound train at Philadelphia one night (incidentally, a N. & W. train) and dropped off at Roanoke early the next morning. Getting quickly to work, in a few days they completed their location surveys and filed maps in each county as required by law. The N. & W. and C. & O. were caught by surprise and could offer no resistance. The railway was organized as the "Tidewater Railway", but when it was nearly completed, Rogers came into the open and consolidated the Deepwater and Tidewater Railways under the name "Virginian Railway".

When the road had been graded, it became necessary to finance track laying. Mr. Rogers had already spent millions, and the "Bankers Panic" of 1907-08 was on. The interests behind the C. & O. and N. & W. tried to prevent Rogers from obtaining the $10,000,000 needed for the tracks and rolling stock, and the banks asked 7% interest. Whereupon John D. Rockefeller, Sr. called a newspaper conference and stated that if his friend H. H. Rogers had any difficulty in obtaining the loan at a reasonable rate, he himself would loan the money. That ended the matter.

In the spring of 1909, Rogers came in his yacht to Norfolk, bringing as guest his friend Mark Twain, to open up the line. Mark Twain declined to leave the yacht, but Mr. Rogers came in his car over the line, stopping at Slab Fork station and having prospective operators to lunch on the car. At the lunch Mr. Rogers announced that he was planning the western extension to the Great Lakes and the purchase of a fleet of steamers to take coal from Norfolk to New York and thus reach the big New York harbor market.

Two weeks later Mr. Rogers dropped dead from a heart attack, and his heirs declined to go forward with his plans.

When Rogers decided to build to Tidewater, he interested a Boston friend and financier, Robert Winsor, in investing in a proposed coal operation on the railway. Winsor was given an option on the 10,000 acre Ellen Smith tract by Beaver Coal Company at $10.00 per acre. This tract later embraced the Slab Fork, Tams, Stotesbury and McAlpin mines. The Beaver Coal Company later sold the timber alone for several times the option price on the whole tract. While considering the option, Winsor's representatives, two young men from Boston named Willoughby Webb and Davenport Brown purchased a two hundred acre piece of bottom land within the Ellen Smith tract as being necessary to the operation of the coal land. When Winsor finally dropped the option, he retained the bottom land. The towns of Tams and Helen were subsequently built on this bottom land.

The final sequel to the story lies in the sale two years ago by the Rogers heirs of the Virginian Railway to the Norfolk and Western Railway.

2

Finances and Organization

At the turn of the century mines could be opened with a relatively small capital investment. All that was required was to build houses for the miners, a store to supply them, and a tipple structure to dump the coal into railway cars. Many companies were organized with no more than $20,000 to $30,000 subscribed by a few men, with the money borrowed from local banks, and the mining company stock put up as collateral. At that date, a "Jenny Lind" three-room house could be erected for $50. No machinery was required in the mine, and the miners furnished their own tools—picks, shovels, breast augers, tamping bars, needles, and axes. The company laid haulage tracks of light steel rails and placed mine cars (usually 1 ton to 2 ton capacity) at the room mouth by mule haulage.

The modest investment required had a profound effect on the development of the coal industry. It made possible, indeed probably inevitable, the establishment of a very large number of companies. Most of these were quite small, and many operated on the traditional shoestring. There can be no question but that the existence of this multitude of small companies greatly speeded the opening of the field. Their officers were able to move quickly and were willing to assume large risks. On the other hand, this fragmentization of the industry placed the average operator very much at the mercy of larger and better financed organizations—railroads, sales companies and, later, labor unions.

When the writer came to West Virginia in 1904, the average cost of producing a long ton (2,240 lbs.) of coal in the Loop Creek section was 85 cents, while the average selling price was about 80 cents. The loss was made up from rents and store profits. The chief users of coal were the railroads (about 28%), domestic users (about 30%), power plants (about 32%), and steel mills (about 10%).

Sales Companies

The many small coal companies had no means of making contact with potential customers. The railways, consequently, felt it necessary to form sales companies in order to insure the movement of coal and thus obtain freight revenue. When J. Pierpont Morgan secured control of the C. & O. Railway, he made Melville E. Ingalls, a Maine lawyer, the president of the road. Mr. Ingalls formed the C. & O. Coal Agency, with his son, George Ingalls, in charge. The agency employed C. B. Orcutt of New York as the eastern manager. He arranged with a Boston coal merchant, P. W. Sprague, to act as New England agent—New England being then the chief market for smokeless coal.

If a coal operator tried to sell his coal without going through the C. & O. Coal Agency, he found it almost impossible to obtain railway cars. The Agency, having no financial interest in the mines, cared little for the coal mines, but a great deal for freight revenue for the railway. The coal was sold, therefore, at a price that barely permitted the mines to survive. In fact, the mines might be said to be in peonage to the railway. The operators in the New River Field finally banded together in a coal sales agency called the New River Consolidated Coal Company and attempted to control the price of their coal. A relative of the writer, Mr. J. Fred Effinger, was president of this company, and the writer once heard him describe how he, accompanied by the freight traffic manager of the C. & O. Railway, called on the Detroit Edison Company and sold them 300,000 tons of coal at a delivered price. Thereupon, Effinger and the railway official went to their hotel and wrangled for two days over the division of the delivered price between the railway and the mines. Published freight rates meant nothing in those days, and rebates were granted on any sizable piece of business.

On the N. & W. Railway a subsidiary of the railway owned most of the coal land, and the railway also organized in 1885 a sales company. Mr. William C. Bullitt (the father of Ambassador Bullitt), a Philadelphia lawyer and a very able and forceful man, was president of this sales company. He later allied himself (1898) with an old Philadelphia coal firm, Castner and Curran. The new firm operated under the name Castner, Curran and Bullitt, and for years all coal produced on the N. & W. Railway was sold by this firm. Coal operators claimed that each year Castner, Curran and Bullitt and the C. & O. Coal Agency got together and decided what was the cheapest price they could allow the operators without breaking them financially.

Just before the beginning of the century, Samuel Dixon on the C. & O. Railway organized the White Oak Coal Company to sell the coal from his mines. About the same time Justus Collins organized the Smokeless Fuel Company, owned largely by himself, to sell the coal from the mines he managed and also coal from the McGuffin mines. The two railway-controlled agencies and the two railways resented these sales companies and harassed them in several ways. However, both survived, and in 1910 the largest company on the N. & W. Railway (the Pocahontas Consolidated Coal Company) formed the Pocahontas Fuel Company and began to sell its own coal. This was followed promptly by other operators, and the complete control of sales by the railways came to an end. The situation never arose on the Virginian Railway, since the problem was solved by the time it began to operate.

In more recent years, the railways have sought other methods of keeping up the volume of coal shipped. Probably the most common device is for a railway, operating through subsidiary companies, to obtain an interest in mines on its lines. Even though a railway might control a number of mines, its real interest remains in hauling coal, not in mining it. If a railway can make a net profit of $1.00 per ton on the hauling of coal, it can obviously afford to lose, if necessary, twenty-five or even fifty cents mining it.

Without doubt it was bad for the coal mining companies, their employees, and the State of West Virginia, that the mines were in the position of being "milk cows" for the railways and the sales companies. To a certain extent this situation still exists, with John L. Lewis now one of the milkers of the cow.

Company Organization

The development of today's vast army of executives and administrators has been a comparatively recent phenomenon in the coal industry. By present standards, the internal organization of the early coal company was simplicity itself. At the turn of the century, the operator was often his own superintendent, salesman, engineer and trouble shooter. His work-week averaged about eighty hours. However, even the most able and zealous operator required help in the form of salaried employees.

The salaried employees were the mine foreman (usually called "bank boss"), the superintendent and the payroll clerk (called "scrip clerk") and store manager and store clerks. The mine foreman received $75 to $100 per month, depending on the size of the mine and number of miners. The superintendent received $100 to $125 per month. The store manager received $75 to $125, and store clerks $40 to $65. Payroll clerks received $40 to $60. At that time, table board cost $18 per month, and salaried employees who were single men were given furnished rooms in the store building without charge. Salaried employees were usually given their store goods at cost. A company that operated several mines employed its own engineer and assistants on salary, usually $75 to $100 per month. Individual mines employed the services of an engineering firm (in the New River and Kanawha fields, the firm of Clark & Krebs).

Land Companies

Approximately ninety percent of the coal produced in Southern West Virginia has been mined from leased land. Much of the best coal land had been purchased by land companies long before profitable mining was possible—that is, before the railroads reached the area. In some cases, the land company had to pay taxes for a decade or more before anyone was willing to take a lease. Among the principal land companies were the Beaver Coal Company, the Flat Top Coal Land Association and the Crozer Land Company.

The standard lease was for a period of thirty years. The lessee had the right to renew for successive thirty-year periods (providing he had complied with all the lease conditions) until the coal was exhausted. The usual lease called for a "royalty" of 10 cents per gross ton mined to be paid by the lessee to the land owner. A few owners, after World War I, made leases calling for a "royalty" of a percentage of the selling price of the coal, f.o.b. mines. However, this proved unworkable, since the lessee could form a company and buy his own coal at a nominal price at the mine and re-sell at the market.

It should be noted that most operators preferred to lease. By the time railway extensions had opened any area for mining, the price of coal lands had risen to a prohibitive level. Indeed, E. J. Berwind was the only large producer who was financially able and willing to purchase land outright.

The Beaver Coal Company

The land companies have played so vital a role in the development of the coal industry that the history of one such company should be recorded. The company selected, the Beaver Coal Company, is far larger than most. However, its methods of operations, leases, etc. were typical. Incidentally, in spite of its name, the Beaver Coal Company never operated a single mine; it was a land company only.

In 1887, certain wealthy men of Philadelphia, including the trustees of the Drexel Estate, sent a young lawyer, Logan M. Bullitt, to Raleigh County to purchase coal land. Starting on Beaver Creek (hence the company name) he and his agent, Azel Ford, purchased a total of about 47,000 acres, ranging from ten acre tracts to the 10,000 acre Ellen Smith tract. The latter tract, containing over 100,000,000 tons of mineable coal in three seams, was purchased in fee for $50,000. The total cost of this 47,000 acres was probably less than $300,000. In 1889 the Beaver Coal Company employed a Philadelphia engineer named Thomas B. Main to survey the property. His chief assistants were John Anderson and E. M. Keatley. They did a splendid job, using survey and prospecting parties, and producing the first accurate map made in Raleigh County. It showed every road and bridle path, every house and log cabin. It also located the outcrop of the No. 5 (Sewell) and No. 3 (Beckley) seams over the entire property, with contour lines of 25 foot intervals, from the creeks up to the outcrop lines. This map was of the greatest value to lessees. It was an amazing performance, since it was made in a country almost without roads and covered by forest, with thickets of laurel in the creek bottoms, and with measurements made on steep hillsides.

Since there was no railway to any part of the property, the land company had to pay taxes and maintain offices in Philadelphia and Beckley for ten years without return. However, in 1898 the Chesapeake and Ohio Railway built the Piney River Branch from Prince to Raleigh. This permitted the lease to the Raleigh Coal Company of 9,000 acres. In 1902, the branch was extended to Mabscott, and the Beckley Coal & Coke Company opened the Beckley Slope mine. In 1907-1908, nearly all of the remaining acreage was leased.

The typical West Virginia lease of that time was used by the Beaver Coal Company. It called for (1) payment of all taxes by the lessee, (2) payment of 10 cents per gross ton for coal mined, (3) payment of $7.50 per acre minimum royalty per annum whether coal was mined or not, (4) use of timber under 10" diameter for mining purposes, and (5) an accurate survey by the lessee of the leased property. After the ten barren years of waiting for railway development, the land company began to reap an excellent and deserved harvest.

Consolidation Effort

At the present time, three large companies —Consolidation Coal Company, Island Creek Coal Company and Winding Gulf Coals, Inc.—produce the greater portion of the smokeless coal tonnage of Southern West Virginia. Fifty years ago, there were probably seventy-five or more separate companies. It may be interesting to rehearse an effort made in 1927-28 to consolidate all the smokeless coal companies in the area.

In 1927, the writer, in conjunction with the Harriman bond house, worked out a plan whereby the smokeless coal mines would be merged into one corporation. Each mine would receive stock in the combined company based on that mine's earning capacity and un-mined coal reserves. When a tentative plan had been worked out, the writer took it to Isaac T. Mann, since he was the head of the largest producing company. Mr. Mann thought well of the plan and called a meeting of operators before whom it was laid. It was decided to explore the idea, and Howard N. Eavenson & Associates of Pittsburgh were employed to make examinations of each company's property, and John Heins & Company of Philadelphia were employed to examine the books of each company and determine their past earning capacities. After months of work, a value was placed on each property by the Eavenson firm, the aggregate totalling about $175,000,000. At the same time General W. J. ("Wild Bill") Donovan, (afterward head of O.S.S. in World War II) was asked for an opinion of the legality of the proposed merger, and gave an approval. The

merger seemed about to succeed, when at the last
moment, a large company in the Pocahontas field
stated that their attorney had advised them their
corporate set-up did not permit them to join the
merger. At the same time several operators in
the Winding Gulf field backed out. While the total tonnage of dissidents did not amount to more
than ten per cent of the total smokeless tonnage,
Mr. Mann was considerably irked at their refusal
and dropped the effort, saying he did not propose
to "hold an umbrella" over the operators who
would not go along. Thus an effort came to
naught that would have stabilized coal mining in
the smokeless field, and would have been of tremendous value during the following years of depression.

3

Work in the Mines
At the Turn of the Century

Coal mining was not a highly skilled occupation. Indeed, a man needed little more than a strong back and average intelligence to become a good miner. The miner often began work as a boy. There were then no minimum age laws, and most companies permitted a boy to work as soon as he was old enough to be useful—twelve to fourteen or so. A boy usually started out as a trapper (opening and closing trap doors between the sections), and often in an area where his father or uncle could keep an eye on him. The fifty cents a day which a boy might earn was an important supplement to many family incomes.

The boy occupied the bottom rung of the mine hierarchy. Above him was the day man. He was usually an older man no longer physically able to load coal, or a youngster not yet experienced enough. The older men usually did track or timber work, while the younger ones drove mules. The day men were paid by the hour. The largest money earners among the miners were the coal loaders. The loaders were paid by the ton or by the mine car, rather than by the hour.

The average miner never became—and rarely aspired to become—more than a good loader. However, an unusually able and ambitious man found no great difficulty in improving his lot. This was especially true in the early days, when new mines were being opened with great rapidity. Operators were always eager to find men competent to serve as foremen.

A Miner's Working Day in 1905

On being employed, the coal loader reported to the payroll clerk (always called "scrip clerk"), who gave him a payroll number and ten round brass checks with his payroll number stamped on them, for which he was charged 10 cents apiece. This was refunded when the loader quit and turned in his checks. The loader carried into the mine his picks, shovels, auger, tamping bar, fuse and a can of black powder. He was charged 50 cents per month for the services of the company blacksmith in re-sharpening and tempering his picks.

The coal loader left his house about 6:00 A. M. If he had left picks at the blacksmith shop the previous evening, he picked them up and walked on into the mine to his working place. He wore a miner's hat with a small lard oil lamp hooked into the hat, and kept at his working place a can of lard oil and cotton wicking. He carried from his house a lunch pail, with food and a water bottle —thermos bottles were not then available.

There were two men at each room face and one man at the narrower entry faces. The man's partner was called his "buddy". If the partner was a beginner learning the ropes, he was called a "back-hand". Many of the foreigners and a few native Americans went into the mine an hour or two before starting time and loaded one or two cars before the other miners arrived.

After taking two-and-a-half to three hours to make an undercut, the miners drilled, loaded, and fired the holes, bringing down the undercut coal. They then pushed up empty mine cars from the room mouth, loaded them, and returned them to the entry. They set the necessary safety props, extended the room track as needed, ate their mid-day meal, and continued until the end of the shift (5:30 p. m.). The miner put his brass check on a hook near the bottom of each car he loaded. The check was removed after the car was dumped at the tipple and the load credited to the proper man. Very occasionally, a thief would dig down into a loaded mine car and replace a check with the thief's own check before the car reached the tip-ple. This was regarded among miners as horse stealing was regarded on the old western frontier.

Mining Methods

At the turn of the century, the average coal mine in Southern West Virginia used no machin-ery inside the mine. The room and pillar method of mining was used, as illustrated by the accom-panying sketch "A". The main haulage road used steel rail of from 16 pounds to the yard weight up to 30 pounds. The cross entries had switch turnouts for each room, made by the company blacksmith. From the switch at the room neck, on up to the face of the room, the track was of wooden rails, 3" x 4", furnished by the company and laid on wood ties, 3" x 4", also furnished by the company. This track was laid by the miner,

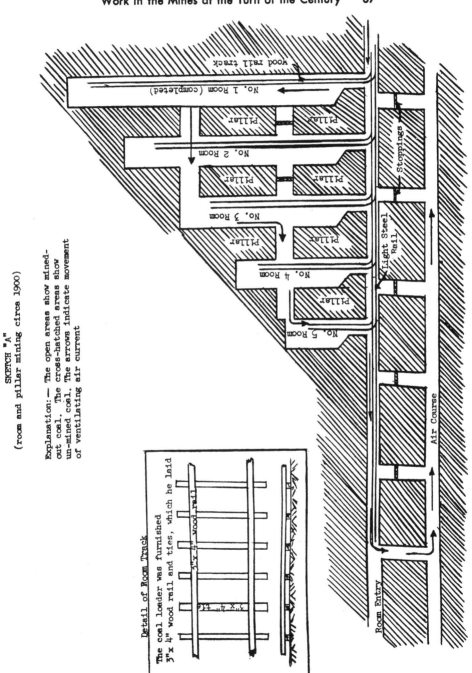

SKETCH "A"
(room and pillar mining circa 1900)

Explanation:— The open areas show mined-
out coal. The cross-hatched areas show
un-mined coal. The arrows indicate movement
of ventilating air current

Detail of Room Track

The coal loader was furnished
3"x 4" wood rail and ties, which he laid

3"x 4" wood rail

3"x 4" tie

Wood rail track

No. 1 Room (completed)

PILLAR   PILLAR

No. 2 Room

PILLAR   PILLAR

No. 3 Room

PILLAR   PILLAR

No. 4 Room

PILLAR

No. 5 Room

Stoppings

Light Steel Rail

Air Course

Room Entry

using his own hammer and saw, and the miner also set his props, with the necessary caps. After the company's track man laid the room switch, the miner furnished all the labor necessary to lay and to advance the track up the room. The cars were placed on the room switch by the company's mule driver and pushed to the face by the miner. The miner then returned the loaded car to the room switch. Sketch "B" shows the method of undercutting, drilling the shot holes, and firing the holes.

The mine haulage was done by mules, although a few mines were experimenting with electric locomotives. The old Pocahontas mine, with 12 foot coal, had coal burning steam locomotives on its main line. In the shaft mines, the mules were kept below for a year. When brought up above ground for a few days of freedom in summer, they were practically blind when first coming into the light.

When cutting machines began to be used, they were, of course, furnished by the company and machine operators, paid by the company, operated the machines and made the cuts. By that time larger cars were used, which required steel rail in the rooms and electric gathering locomotives (operating by a reel cable hooked to the trolley wire on the entry) to place the empty cars at the room face and to pull the loaded cars from the room face to the entry.

The first machines were operated by compressed air, and consisted of drills which punched undercuts similar to hand-dug cuts. These were soon superseded by electrically operated cutting

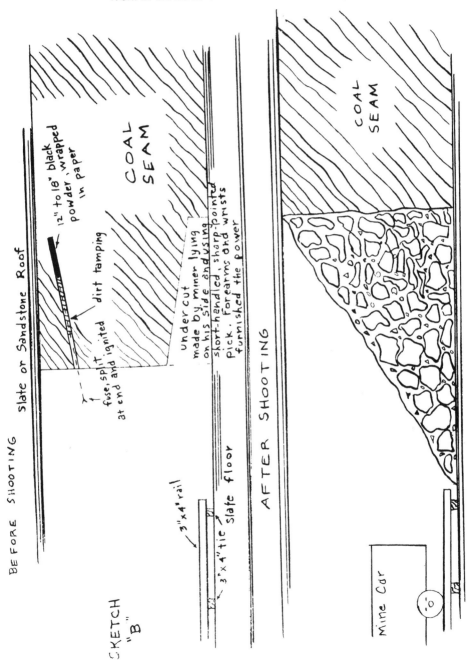

SKETCH "B"

BEFORE SHOOTING   Slate or Sandstone Roof

12" to 18" black wrapped powder, wrapped in paper

dirt tamping

fuse, split at end and ignited

COAL SEAM

undercut made by miner lying on his side and using short-handled, sharp-pointed pick. Forearms and wrists furnished the power.

3" x 4" rail

3" x 4" tie   slate floor

AFTER SHOOTING

COAL SEAM

Mine Car

machines. In the old days, two miners, working in a room 24 feet wide, required 2½ to 3 hours to complete a cut 5 feet deep. The electric cutting machine made a cut six feet deep across a thirty foot room in 30 minutes. These machines were operated on the night shift, and miners working on the day shift had only to shoot down and load the coal.

At the present time, machines are used not only to undercut the coal but to load the coal on to conveyors or into shuttle cars carrying the coal to the entry. It is there dumped on to belt conveyors which discharge into cars or on to main line belt conveyors. Where the coal is thick enough, so-called "continuous miners" are now used. These consist of boring machines which cut cylindrical holes into the coal face and discharge the coal so dug behind the machine on to a conveyor. At the turn of the century the daily output per mine varied from 200 tons to the Sun Mine's 1,800 tons, with an average of probably 800 tons. Today the output varies from 800 tons to 10,000 tons daily per mine.

Hours

In 1904 the mines operated on a ten hour day at the working place, commencing at 7:00 A. M. and ending at 5:30 P. M., with a half hour off for lunch. In the winter of 1911-12, the writer changed his mines from the ten hour day to the nine hour day, without any reduction in the daily pay. No effort was made to get the agreement of other operators before doing this, since I felt sure they would not agree. However, I also felt sure they would recognize an accomplished fact, and after a certain amount of criticism, would follow suit. That is what happened. The Winding Gulf Operators followed suit almost immediately and the other fields in a few months.

When our country entered World War I, the price of coal had risen very high, and every mine was making money. President Wilson asked business and labor not to try to alter the status quo in any industry. In other words, unionized fields were to stay unionized, and unions were not to try to organize non-union areas. In view of this situation, it seemed good sense for the non-union coal fields to go to the 8 hour day and to pay an equal or greater wage scale than the unionized fields. This was done in all the southern West Virginia coal fields.

Wages

In 1904 the average wage for a day man was two dollars; a loader might make three dollars or more, depending on his industry. Men were paid the last Saturday in the month for the preceding month. The native white Americans usually drew a fair amount of cash wages, the Negroes had generally eaten up their credit at the store, while the foreigners, used to frugal living in their home lands, usually drew sizeable amounts at pay days.

The southern West Virginia coal fields continued to pay better wages than the union fields and remained non-union until the depression of 1929. During the period 1930-1932, many of the mines in this area cut wages and increased the working hours. Thus, when President Roosevelt urged all workers to join unions, the UMWA had little difficulty in organizing these fields. Those operators who had attempted to maintain living wages during the depression came to the regretful conclusion that only the union could keep their unfair competitors in line.

Labor Relations

During the first thirty years of mining in Southern West Virginia, efforts to organize mines were sporadic and more or less limited to the separate coal fields. When John Mitchell and his UMWA called the 1902 anthracite strike, the Kanawha field was organized and the New River field partly organized. When, as a result of President Roosevelt's intervention, the strike was settled, the Kanawha field remained organized (excepting the Cabin Creek section), but the rest of Southern West Virginia was non-union.

In an agreement made by the Central Competitive Field (Pennsylvania, Ohio, Indiana and Illinois) with the UMWA in the early part of this century, the union agreed to organize the southern coal fields, including Southern West Virginia. Later, the Southern West Virginia operators brought suit against the UMWA on the ground that they had entered into a conspiracy with Northern operators to put the Southern operators out of business, and obtained an injunction against the UMWA. An effort in 1912 to organize Cabin Creek resulted in so much violence that the National Guard was called out and a Congressional Committee investigated the situation. When Governor Henry D. Hatfield assumed office in 1913, he not only settled the strike but also initiated the "Workman's Compensation Department", long needed in the State and accepted without opposition by coal operators. The general labor situation remained little changed until World War I.

When the United States entered the war in April 1917, President Wilson requested a truce in labor warfare—organized industries were to remain organized and vice versa. Shortly after the end of the war, the UMWA made an effort to organize the New River and Winding Gulf Fields. When violence seemed imminent, Governor Cornwell requested the Federal Government to send troops, and a battalion of the First Division was sent from Kentucky and camped on the outskirts of Beckley. This ended the threatened trouble.

In 1922, the UMWA called a strike in the anthracite fields and shortly after called a strike of bituminous miners in support of the anthracite strike. This strike lasted seven months. Only the coal mines south of the Potomac and Ohio rivers remained at work and enabled the nation's industries to operate. Naturally, the price of coal began to leap upward, and Herbert Hoover, then Secretary of Commerce, called a meeting of operators in Washington and asked that a maximum price be agreed to. This request was accepted by the operators, and a runaway market was brought under control. The prices suggested by Mr. Hoover were adopted.

The Southern West Virginia mines were now working an eight hour day and paying higher wages than the union scale, and no serious effort was made to organize the mines. When the 1929 depression commenced, the organized mines in the north began to fall away from the UMWA, and by 1932 only the anthracite area of Pennsylvania and the State of Illinois remained in the union fold. The UMWA was reduced to less than 100,000 dues paying members.

When F. D. Roosevelt assumed office in 1933, John L. Lewis borrowed several hundred thousand dollars from the American Federation of Labor and commenced a vigorous campaign to organize the non-union mines. Due to the policy of wage-cutting during the depression, and with the aid of the Administration, this was accomplished. Congress passed, at Roosevelt's request, the N. I. R. A. Act, and the coal operators of the Appalachian area were required to meet the Administrator, General Hugh Johnson, and the UMWA representatives to agree on a code. The southern operators appointed James D. Francis and Ralph Taggart, and the northern operators appointed Charles O'Neill of Central Pennsylvania and John D. Morrow of the Pittsburgh Coal Company. This group wrangled for months before agreeing on a code fixing wages, working conditions, and prices. General Johnson was a colorful character, an ex-cavalryman who liked to consider himself a tough, top-sergeant type. The operators of Indiana and Illinois and the far west resented the fixing of conditions by the Appalachian operators but were helpless in the matter.

From this point onward, the UMWA demanded and received increases in wages every year or two. During World War II, they called strikes several times and were given what they demanded by Secretary Ickes, who was Fuel Administrator. Shortly after the end of the war the Union demanded "portal to portal" pay, which meant pay for the time required to reach their working places. A law-suit developed on this point, and the case was tried in Federal Court before Judge A. D. Barksdale. The suit was won by the coal operators. However, the Union appealed, and had Barksdale reversed by the Appellate Court. The operators then carried it to the Supreme Court and lost.

The present method of dealing with the UMWA is through two associations: the Bituminous Coal Operators Association consisting of Ohio, Pennsylvania, Northern West Virginia, and a certain number of Southern West Virginia operators, and the other a group of Southern West Virginia and Kentucky operators, called the Southern Coal Operators Association. The UMWA usually makes an agreement with the Bituminous Operators Association first and then presents the agreement to the other association for signature. "DIVIDE ET IMPERA". Mr. Lewis has studied history and knows the Latin motto.

Welfare Fund

One of Mr. Lewis' demands during World War II was a contribution by the operators to a welfare fund for miners. This was finally agreed to, and in a few years has been advanced to forty cents per ton. As a concession to public opinion, the fund is supposed to be administered by three people: a representative of labor, of the operators and of the "public". Since Mr. Lewis appointed his employee, Miss Josephine Roche, as public representative (on the ground that she had once been Assistant Secretary of the Treasury, under Roosevelt), he naturally controls the Board. If the operator representative objects to any proposed action, or suggests an action not agreeable to the UMWA, the other two members simply out-vote him.

However, in all fairness, it must be said that Mr. Lewis has not abused his power. The fund is honestly and economically administered, and it is understood that Mr. Lewis does not accept a salary from the fund. Miners' hospitals have been built throughout the coal area, with highly paid and competent medical and surgical personnel. Particular attention is given to paraplegic cases —the all too common result of mining injuries. The fund also pays pensions to retired miners.

Two Labor Episodes

The late P. M. Snyder of Mount Hope related the following occurrence to the writer. About the turn of the century, an effort was made in Fayette County to organize the miners. General J. W. St. Clair, an outstanding lawyer, was engaged by the union organizers to represent them. Coming to Macdonald, on Loop Creek, to address the miners, he spoke from a platform erected beside the railway track. This was just below the hill on which Mr. Samuel Dixon, operator of Macdonald mine, lived. While General St. Clair was delivering an impassioned harangue on the rights of the miners and how he proposed to fight for those rights,

Mr. Dixon was lurking in the laurel thicket near the platform. As soon as General St. Clair finished his speech, Mr. Dixon leaped upon the platform, rushed over to the General, congratulated him on the speech and said, "We are waiting dinner for you, General, up at my house. Come right along up." Whereupon, the audience of miners muttered "sold out again", and the meeting broke up and so did the effort to organize.

*   *

At the time John Mitchell called the anthracite strike on April 1st, 1902, the market for smokeless coal in the New River field was depressed. As smokeless coal began to be used as a substitute for anthracite, the market began to pick up but was still not good as to price. Mitchell decided to call a strike in the Southern West Virginia smokeless fields as of June 15th to support his anthracite strike. The New River operators decided not to combat the strike in view of the low price of coal at the moment. However, Mr. Justus Collins had other ideas. On the morning the strike was to commence, he brought some forty armed Baldwin-Felts men, equipped with a gatling gun and a search-light, into Thurmond and up Loop Creek to his mine at Glen Jean. The gatling gun and the search-light were mounted on the tipple, where they commanded the mine and town. The armed men patrolled the borders of the mine property, preventing any trespassing. When the Collins miners saw they were protected from threats and molestation by strikers from other mines, they went to work. Men from the struck mines also came to the Collins mine, and soon the mine was producing two thousand tons per day. With the price of coal mounting rapidly, Collins was making a handsome profit. The other New River operators, with their mines struck, were not able to break the strike and resume operation for several months.

Explosions

The Southern West Virginia coal fields have suffered their share of mine disasters. The first occurred more than sixty years ago in the original Pocahontas mine. In the New River field, there were serious explosions at Red Ash (1900), Rush Run (1905), Parral (1906), Stuart (1907), and Whipple (1907). In the Pocahontas field, Lick Branch and Haveco had explosions, and, on the Virginian Railway, the Eccles mine twice blew up with severe loss of life (183 men were killed in the explosion on April 28, 1914). A mine explosion always created a pitiful situation, especially at a shaft mine. The approaches to the shaft were roped off, and deputy sheriffs had to keep onlookers back of the rope to prevent interference with rescue operations. It was a very moving sight to see the women with shawls over their heads and babies in their arms, asking eagerly each rescue team as they came up out of the blown-up pit,—"have you seen my man?"

Any error in judgment or procedure on the part of a single miner could cause a tragedy. The explosion at the Stuart (Lochgelly) mine on January 29, 1907 may serve as an example. Dick Lee, an old Negro miner from Alabama with many years experience, worked in a room on the 3rd left entry, off of the entry being driven towards Parral. When we were cleaning up the mine after the explosion, Lee's body was found in the room. The evidence was plain that he had drilled and loaded three holes "on the solid", and had fired the first one, tamped with coal dust instead of clay, and not sufficient coal dust at that. This had resulted in a "blown out" shot, which back-fired, stirred up and ignited coal dust, and generated an explosion which "snow-balled" as it spread through the mine and killed every living thing. It was not a gas explosion.

The sight at the shaft bottom when we got down was pitiful. Over fifty men were lying dead. My transit man for the Stuart and Parral mines, Jesse Arthur, was lying on a mine locomotive with the top of his head blown off. One of the men was sitting with his back against the coal rib, his lunch bucket between his legs, and a piece of bread in his mouth, held by his hand.

On the side of the shaft opposite the side where the explosion originated, a few men lived a minute or so before "afterdamp" killed them. One Polish miner had evidently been able to get from the face of his room a hundred feet down towards the entry before the "afterdamp" got him. We found him kneeling in prayer against the room rib. With his hand he had made the Sign of the Cross in the coal dust on the rib.

In 1907, after a number of mine explosions, the Federal Government organized through the Bureau of Mines the study of mine disasters and of possible preventive measures. When the Whipple mine blew up in the spring of 1907, the Bureau sent a young engineer named George S. Rice to accompany the rescue and clean up parties and learn how it was done. The writer, as a fellow engineer, was given the job of taking him along and explaining procedures. Mr. Rice eventually became Chief Mining Engineer of the Bureau of Mines.

In the early days gas, called "fire damp" (a name inherited from British miners) which is methane, CH_4 was believed to be the sole cause of all explosions. The fact is that the gas acts usually only as a detonator, stirring up and exploding coal dust. After cutting machines were introduced, coal dust became far more prevalent in the mines than in pick mining days, and a great source of danger. Paradoxically enough, the introduction of very large ventilating fans fifty years ago created a danger, because the large volume of air circulated by these fans served to dry out the coal dust and make it all the more dangerous. The introduction of rock-dusting has been a great means of lessening the danger of dust explosions and of limiting their scope.

Roof falls are less spectacular than explosions and do not make newspaper headlines, but they are the cause of more injuries and fatalities. This source of accident has been largely controlled in late years by roof-bolting; i. e. using steel bolts to fasten the loose slate immediately over the coal seam to the more solid slate or rock above. However, in spite of the United States Bureau of Mines and the excellent State Department of Mines, coal mining has remained a hazardous occupation.

4

Life in the Coal Fields
At the Turn of the Century

The company town and the company store
have long been favorite targets of critics of the
coal industry. Many appear to have believed that
both were imposed on helpless miners by rapacious operators. However, such a view reveals a
complete misunderstanding of the situation. In
point of fact, the operators built towns because
they had no alternative. The mining of coal re-
quires miners; miners require houses. Since most
mines were opened in virtually unsettled areas,
there was no existing housing. Thus new houses
had to be built, and the operators were the only
ones with the capital and organization to do the
job. Since the almost complete absence of all-
weather roads made it necessary for the miner
to live close to his work, small villages (often
called "camps") were built close to each mine.

The average monthly rent of a miner's house
was $1.50 per room for a "Jenny Lind" type of
house, consisting of boards and battens outside,
and ceiling boards inside; and $2.00 per room for
a house weather-boarded outside and plastered
inside. There was hardly any variation from these
figures. The coal operator had to maintain the
house, replace broken windows, mend leaky roofs,
and repaint from time to time.

The newly arrived miners and their families required not only housing but also food, clothing, etc., as well as powder, fuse and caps. However, in most cases there were no stores within reasonable distance, and it often required the better part of a day to visit one. During bad weather it was often impossible to do so at all. Thus, a store in each mining community was essential, and the operator was usually the only one with sufficient capital to provide it.

Much misunderstanding has been circulated —often deliberately—about the operation of the company store. The true situation was quite different. As a convenience to the miner and his family, credit was extended by issuing orders on the store in the form of scrip. It should be stressed that at least in "my" area no one was required to ask for scrip. All employees could make their purchases in cash if they so desired. Indeed, many miners, especially the foreign born, never drew scrip. The profits made by the company stores varied widely. Some companies took advantage of a near-monopoly, and charged all the traffic would bear. However, others—including those controlled by the writer—operated on a profit margin considerably below that general among "private" stores in the area. In short, the company stores deserved only a fraction of the abuse hurled against them. However, it was a cheap and easy trick for union organizers or for competing and envious merchants to brand the company store as a "robber." Human nature being what it is, men who were careless in money matters and who let themselves get into debt eased their consciences by joining in the name calling.

Many coal companies built churches and

school buildings at each mining camp, and often supplemented the five or six months of schooling furnished by the county with an additional two or three months. The services of a company doctor were charged to each employee at 50 cents per month for single men and $1.00 per month for married men. Delivery of babies cost $5.00, and medicine was included in the doctor's charge. By the time of World War I, the charges had gone up to $1.00 for single men and $2.00 for married men. Usually one doctor (with an assistant paid a small salary by the doctor) served two or three mines, traveling by horseback from mine to mine.

Travel

It may be of interest to describe local travel conditions in this area in the early part of this century. The roads were, of course, unpaved and impassable to wheeled traffic in the winter months. The writer remembers keenly his first trip to Beckley from Mt. Hope in the winter of 1905. On horse back, with the horse's tail tied up to keep it out of the mud, it took three hours to cover the eleven miles of road (now covered in fifteen minutes). On entering the village of Beckley, then eight hundred people, several wagons were to be seen, mired in the mud. The owners had unhitched their teams, and would return in the spring, hitch up, and take the wagons home. Beckley lawyers who had cases at the Fayetteville bar (a distance by road of about twenty-five miles) would have to take the early morning train from Beckley Junction down to Prince, then the C. & O. Railway local train to Fayette Station, thence by a four mile road up the mountain to Fayetteville.

Anyone who had to go from, say, Macdonald to Bluefield, had to take the early morning Loop Creek branch line train down to Thurmond, then the C. & O. Railway mainline train to Huntington, then a local train to Kenova, and get the N. & W. Railway train to Bluefield. The whole trip used up nearly two days. Today it can be done by automobile in two hours or so.

For movement from mine to mine, the New River Company, under Mr. Dixon, used four wheeled track bicycles propelled by pedals. These were furnished to management officials who had to go to all mines and to the engineers. The latter used double track bicycles, with two seats side by side and a wire basket in front to carry transits and other survey impedimenta. To pump one of these bicycles up a two or three per cent grade required considerable leg power. The writer, who had to use them constantly, had legs of iron as a result. Mr. Dixon thought nothing of travelling in the morning from Macdonald to Stuart, a distance of fifteen miles, stopping at each mine on the way, and returning to Macdonald in the afternoon. He also thought nothing of requiring the same exertion from subordinates. Of course after hard surfaced roads came into use, these bicycles were relegated to the scrap pile. The writer had one in use on the Winding Gulf branch of the C. & O. Railway until about 1922.

The first automobile in Fayette County was purchased in 1912 by S. A. Scott, then head of the New River Company, who used it between his house at Prudence and his office at Macdonald. The first car in Raleigh County was purchased in 1910 by William MacTaggart, superintendent of the Beaver Coal Company. He drove one day from Beckley to Tams, where it practically laid the mine down, as all the people quit work to follow it up and down the town. MacTaggart was unable to get it back from Tams to the top of the mountain, and we had to hitch one of our mule teams to it and haul it up, and request him not to repeat the trip—very politely, because he was the representative of our landlord.

Recreation

There were no movies, radios, or automobiles in those days, and almost the only amusement for the men were the saloons, of which there was at least one at each camp of any size in Fayette County. Raleigh County was officially dry, but in actual practice quite wet indeed. Each Saturday what was known as the "Fanny Train" would arrive in Prince loaded with liquor to be sold to miners. In addition to this "legal liquor," there was generally a plentiful supply of moonshine available for those with an adventuresome spirit.

In the small village of Mount Hope, where the writer lived for several years, there were eight saloons. In those halcyon days, whiskey was 10 cents a drink and a full quart bottle was $1.00. On pay days, professional gamblers from Cincinnati came to Mount Hope bringing their paraphernalia with them and set up faro, roulette, chuck-a-luck, birdcage, etc. games in the back rooms of the saloons. They reaped a golden harvest from the miners The operators and salaried men who enjoyed games of chance pursued them in the somewhat more comfortable atmosphere of the Dunglen Hotel at Thurmond. Even here, one took one's chances. In a poker game at the Dunglen, one of the Ash family held three red cards and two black cards, of four different suits. He claimed the pot. An opponent, holding threes, objected and asked Ash what he claimed his hand to be. Ash replied, "it is a Mud River full house, and it takes the pot." Since Ash was police chief of Thurmond, was six feet three inches tall, weighed 275 pounds, and his opponent weighed 150 pounds, Ash took the pot.

There was each Sunday at Glen Jean on Loop Creek, except in winter, a battle between a wild cat and a bull terrier. The dog had to kill the cat in ten minutes or be declared the loser. Such contests were enjoyed both as spectacles and as opportunities to gamble. The writer once owned one of the bull terriers which had been in such fights, and his muzzle and neck were scarred from his battles. However, the church women of the community put up such a fight against this amusement that the county authorities had to stop it.

In the New River field baseball was a passion, and Loop Creek always had a good team. At Glen Jean on Loop Creek, William McKell built a baseball field with a grandstand on the third base side, seating several hundred people. Some outstanding players were Bill Farrell, a C. & O. Railway employee, Charley Middleberg, a West Virginia University athlete, and Bill Davidson, the Armour Company representative. Among the teams regularly played by Loop Creek

were the House of David, whose members wore
their hair down to their waists (Grover Alexander, the National League star, was a member
of this team in his last days) and Green's Ne-
braska Indians. The latter team was made up of
genuine Indians except Green, who was manager.
The purpose of the team was to "plug" Green's
patent medicine, and Green would go through the
spectators before the game begging everyone to
buy the medicine for "the insignificant, micro-
scopical, pusillanimous, sum of a dime, ten cents."

Among the players developed in the field,
three reached the big leagues: "Sheriff" Blake,
of an old Fayette County family, Jerry Hofer of
Mt. Hope, and Harry Moran of Anstead. All of
them got homesick for West Virginia and did not
stay long in the big leagues. They were all pitch-
ers and good ones too, as this writer can testify
from having batted against Hofer and Moran.
Harry Moran is now a coal operator in Beckley,
and pitches curves against business opponents as
effectively as he used to do against batters. From
big league pitcher down to coal operator—how
are the mighty fallen!

Baseball games could be exciting affairs indeed. On one occasion a group of school boys from
Virginia came to Glen Jean to play the Loop
Creek team. They had been filled with stories of
how rough the coal fields were and were rather
nervous. During the game a dispute arose between
two Baldwin-Felts deputy sheriffs. One of them,
M. L. Parker from Buena Vista, Virginia, was
betting on the Virginia school boys; the other,
Vic Rudd from Huntington, was backing Loop
Creek. The argument reached the fighting point,

and each reached for his gun. Rudd got his gun
out first, while Parker's stuck in his hip pocket,
so Parker had to retreat down the third base line,
bending over. Rudd's shot grazed Parker's back,
damaging his coat. Parker then got his gun out,
turned and fired, catching Rudd in the mouth and
ruining a new pair of dental plates. During the
excitement, John Wilson, assistant manager of
the New River Company, a small man weighing
115 pounds, claimed he got behind a 4 inch by 4
inch post for protection, and that Dr. Gory Hogg,
weighing 220 pounds, got behind him! In the
meantime, the Virginia school boys had disappeared over the fence, convinced that they were
being shot at. When finally rounded up and in-
duced to resume play, they were so nervous that
they were easily beaten. Rudd and Parker were
persuaded to shake hands, and everyone ad-
journed to Deegans saloon near the C. & O. Railway station—as was usual after a game.

Law and Order

The early miners were a hard-bitten lot.
During the election week of 1904 eight men (including Sheriff Daniel) were killed in Fayette
County. Brawls, often ending in serious injury
or even death, were a common occurrence. These
were treated quite casually by the authorities.
At Thurmond there was a railway bridge across
New River from the C. & O. Railway main line
over to the south side, which carried a road-
way beside the railway tracks. To walk across
late at night was a somewhat hazardous pro-
ceeding. One morning after pay day, an un-
identified body was found on the walkway of the

bridge, obviously murdered. The mayor of Thurmond held an inquest on the body, on which was found $48.00. He assessed a fine of $20.00 for committing suicide and $28.00 costs. The fine was used for burying the body.

To preserve some semblance of order in the camps and on the branch line passenger trains, deputy sheriffs were employed. These men were deputized by the county sheriff but paid by the coal operators, since the counties were not financially able to assume the burden. As might be imagined, these guards were rough and often colorful individuals. Some fifty years ago, the Slab Fork Coal Company employed as police officer Captain Nat Ressler, a noted marksman. He had travelled the vaudeville circuit giving amazing exhibitions, such as shooting over his shoulder—using a knife blade as a mirror—and hitting a match held by his wife in her mouth. One night at Slab Fork mine a small carnival show was being held, and a young colored fellow with too much liquor in him was causing trouble. Ressler ordered him to behave, but when he turned his back to go away, the youth drew a gun and fatally shot Ressler, who fell to the ground. He was able to get his gun out, however, and shot his assailant who had gotten fifty feet away and was running (a difficult target for an uninjured man) and killed him instantly. Ressler died on the train taking him to the hospital at Princeton.

All the Baldwin-Felts deputies were good shots—they had to be. The youngest of the Felts brothers, Albert, won the police championship. However, two of the Hatfield clan, Troy and Elias, who were with the Baldwin-Felts Agency for a while, were probably the best shots in an actual shooting affray. The writer once saw Troy Hatfield cut a designated leaf from a tree with a pistol shot, and also hit a tossed up silver dollar. These two brothers ended up as police officers for the Boomer Coal Company, on Kanawha River, where there was a large company town. An Italian living at Boomer was causing trouble by bootlegging liquor, and Elias and Troy Hatfield were asked by the management to put him off the job. Not expecting any resistance, the two officers went to the Italian's house, one going to the front door and the other to the back. When the brother at the front door knocked, the Italian suddenly opened the door and shot him dead. The other Hatfield, thinking his brother had done the shooting, came around to the front and was shot through the heart by the Italian. As he fell he drew his gun, shot and killed the Italian and died himself.

The employment of company-paid deputies was outlawed by the Legislature in 1935. However, by that time there were relatively few of them left. The development of good roads and the resulting ability of the State Police to get to the mines quickly had made them unnecessary. Then too, those same good roads made it possible for the miner to live some miles from the mine. Slowly but surely, the isolated mine camps began to disappear. Their shabby, unpainted ruins are a common and depressing feature of the local landscape.

Foreign-Born Miners

The mines first employed native labor. However, the sparsely settled region could not provide an adequate labor supply, and miners were soon brought in from Pennsylvania and Virginia. When it became necessary to get additional labor into the coal fields, an easily available source of Negro labor was on hand in Virginia and North Carolina. A great deal of this labor was secured by men, already working in the mines, writing home to friends asking them to come out. In times of great shortages of labor, such as in strikes, an agent would be sent to the states named, and would collect ten to fifty men and bring them out to the mines by railway. This was spoken of as bringing men in "on transportation". The cost of transporting these men was charged against them and collected from their first few months wages. Naturally, many of them slipped away— either back home or to some other mine—to escape paying their railway fare. Generally speaking, "transportation" labor was not very efficient and did not compare with labor brought in by invitation of friends already employed.

Up until World War I, the steamship companies brought millions of men into the country as steerage passengers at very low rates. These men came chiefly from the Austro-Hungarian Empire. They went to work in heavy industries, such as steel mills and coal mines, and were excellent workers. Hard as life might be in the mills and mines, it was generally far easier than it had been in their home land. Such men worked hard, saved money, and as soon as possible sent back for their families. The following description of their way of living at a coal mine is typical of this group.

A man who had brought his wife with him would rent a four room house from the coal company. One room was used as a kitchen and eating room. The man, his wife and children occupied a second room. The other two rooms had four beds each, and eight men would sleep in each room. The woman would cook and wash for all the men, dividing up the cost of food and charging each man, including her husband, an equal part of the entire cost. The husband did, however, get his laundry done free.

There were no bath houses at the mines, and the miner coming home from work knelt down over a tub of hot water, while his wife scrubbed him off with a brush. The writer is proud to say he built the first miners' bath house in these fields in 1910.

On pay day the household joined in the purchase of beer. This was poured into a galvanized iron tub, and the night was spent in drinking and singing songs of the old country. The various Saints Days—called "Big Sundays"—were also occasions for celebration. However, with these exceptions, the majority of foreign miners devoted themselves to work and family. As a group, they spent far less on liquor and gambling than either the Negroes or the white Americans.

When the woman of the house gave birth to a baby, she would take a maximum of three days off from housekeeping, and the husband would stop work for that period and do the cooking. The foreign woman did not wear shoes except in very cold weather and wore inexpensive clothes such as were used in the old country. The children of these foreign-born miners quickly learned English at the public school, and the girls were used by their mothers to do the shopping and wherever translation was necessary. By the time the children were grown, they could still understand their parent's language, but many had lost the ability to speak it. These foreigners made good miners, worked hard and saved their money. Their contribution to the development of both the coal industry and the State was great indeed.

5

The Gulf Smokeless Coal Company

In the preceding chapters I have attempted to outline something of the history and development of the Southern West Virginia smokeless coal fields. There seems some merit in supplementing this rather general discussion with a more detailed examination of a single coal company. For this "case study" I have naturally selected the company with which I am most familiar—the Gulf Smokeless Coal Company.

In 1905, while employed as engineer by Samuel Dixon, I noticed from maps available that the Beckley seam of coal appeared to thicken towards the Winding Gulf section in Raleigh County. Since coal seams occur in elongated lenses, it could be supposed that the Winding Gulf was the long axis of the lens of the Beckley seam. Accordingly, I made a horseback trip in December 1905 to Raleigh County, where I picked up a man who had made openings in the Beckley seam for the land-owning Beaver Coal Company. We prospected the Winding Gulf Creek, which is one of the headwaters of the Guyan River, and found the Beckley seam to occur there as a double seam. The top bench had a thickness of six feet, and, separated by a parting of ten inches to eighteen inches, a lower bench of three feet. I then asked my relative, J. Fred Effinger of Staunton, Virginia, who was a college class-mate of William C. Bullitt, the president of the Beaver Coal Company, to try to get the promise of a lease on the Winding Gulf whenever the area should be opened by a railway. Mr. Bullitt agreed to give us a three thousand acre lease. My friend, James O. Watts of Lynchburg, Virginia, also at the time in the employ of Mr. Dixon, was associated with me in the proposed lease.

In 1908 the Beaver Coal Company demanded that the lease be signed at once, obligating the lessee to pay annual royalties, without any railway having been built into the Winding Gulf and without any assurance of a railway in the near future. My elderly relative, Mr. Effinger and Watt's father, both men of considerable means, refused to obligate themselves under such conditions, especially as the "Bankers Panic" of 1907-08 was still in effect. Watts and I, being young men, wanted to go ahead but needed the moral support of an older and more experienced coal man. I therefore put the proposition to our employer, Mr. Dixon, who with his usual quick decisiveness said "you have a good thing and I will back you—go ahead." We then got a charter, signed the lease, and organized a company under the name of "The New River Coal and Coke Company", changed a year later to "Gulf Smokeless Coal Company". Fortunately for us, the Virginian Railway decided, late in 1908, to build a branch from their main line at Mullens up the Winding Gulf, a distance of 24 miles. Construction began in November.

I at once moved to Slab Fork, rented a house

from Mr. Caperton, and commenced a survey of the lease, walking two miles over the mountain from Slab Fork to the Winding Gulf each day, doing a day's survey work, and walking back in the evening. By the spring of 1909, I was able to get materials hauled over the mountain from Slab Fork to our lease on the Gulf and erected the cottage (in which I still live) and which served as a dwelling and an office for eighteen months. I had contracted with the owner of a circular sawmill to bring his mill to the proposed town site. In April 1909 the mill started operation and we commenced to build the town and the tipple and to open the coal seam.

As organized, the company had a capital of $200,000, with Mr. Samuel Dixon as president, myself as vice president and general manager, and James O. Watts as secretary and treasurer. We levied assessments of ten per cent on the stockholders as the money was needed. It may be of interest to note that we paid our first dividend in 1910, the month after we had levied the last ten per cent assessment. As a comparison, it may be mentioned that of our neighbors, Mac-Alpin Coal Company, with a 1700 acre lease, had a capital of $100,000, E. E. White Coal Company, with 5000 acres, a capital of $500,000 (of which $50,000 was bonus stock), and Bailey-Wood Coal Company, with 600 acres, a capital of $50,000. When my cousin, J. Fred Effinger, my father, Ferdinand Howald, and two other stockholders opened Rush Run mine in 1887, the capital stock was $20,000, but since that time electric haulage had been introduced. This required wiring, electric locomotives and power plants.

The Virginian Railway track did not reach our mine until October 1st, 1909, on which date we loaded and shipped our first car of coal. At first, we had to slide the coal down the side of the mountain in a chute and wheel it over to our side track in a push car. Since we were unable to get the machinery for the permanent tipple until the railway had reached us, it was not until April 1910 that we could get our permanent tipple in operation. After that we increased production from 3,000 tons per month in March to 30,-000 tons in September.

Starting construction of the town in May 1909, we completed 125 houses within one year. The frame lumber for the houses and the lumber for the tipple was sawed from the timber growing on the town site. These houses consisted of three and four rooms, plastered inside and weatherboarded outside, and painted. The town was divided into three sections. The houses above the tipple were occupied by the Negroes, the section below the tipple by white Americans, and still further down a section for the foreign miners. All the houses were exactly alike, with no facilities in any one section that were not available in the other sections. By this time we had 300 men working in the mine, tipple and town. In November 1910, we completed the store and office building. At this time, the town water supply was furnished by driven wells with hand pumps, one well to each 8 houses, and electric lights had been installed in each house. In 1913, a large well was sunk at the power house and a filtered water system placed in operation, with running water available in each house. This system is still (1963) in operation. Additional houses were built from time to time as needed, until the last houses were built in 1920. This brought the total dwellings to 185. It is estimated that there was an average of seven men, women and children per house in the colored section of 75 houses; five per house in the white American section of 75 houses; and ten per house in the foreign section of 35 houses, making a total of 1,250 people.

By way of comparison, the county seat of Beckley had a population of only 800 at that time, and did not have a piped water system, electric lights, or a moving picture theatre until after our town had them. If the people of Beckley wished to see a circus, they had to come to Tams to do so. In 1910 we put in bath houses for the miners—then a novelty at coal mines—and in 1911 built the first movie theatre at any mine in West Virginia.

In 1912 the Gulf Coal Company, with a mine named Hotcoal located four miles above Tams, offered to sell the property to the writer. This offer was accepted, and Gulf Coal Company was operated as a separate company with the writer as operating head. At this time, Mr. Samuel Dixon sold his stock in Gulf Smokeless Coal Company to James O. Watts and the writer, and I was made president and general manager. The Hotcoal mine produced about 600 tons per day and proved very profitable.

In 1914 the Wyoming Land Company (a subsidiary of the Virginian Railway) offered the writer a lease of 3000 acres nine miles below Tams, on the Winding Gulf. The Wyoming Coal Company was organized with a capital of $100,-

000 (afterward increased to $135,000) to operate this lease, and production of coal began in 1915. The tonnage from this property increased ultimately to 1,400 tons per day.

When World War I began in August 1914, coal business was very adversely affected. The Tams, Hotcoal, and Wyco mines could not find a market for coal sufficient to operate more than three days per week. This condition persisted until the fall of 1916, when the situation suddenly reversed and a runaway market developed in the spring of 1917.

In the meantime, in 1913, the Gulf Smokeless Coal Company leased ground at their Norfolk terminal from the Virginian Railway and built a 50,000 ton capacity storage plant there. This allowed us to store coal in the dull summer market and re-load and sell it in the winter. When this country entered the war in April 1917, this storage plant was turned over to the Navy Department, which at that time burned smokeless coal exclusively.

During the war, the coal mines of the country were under the control of the Fuel Administration as to prices, markets, and wages. During this period the writer was absent in the army. The three mines were operated by J. W. Wilson, who had been assistant general manager.

In 1919, the Covel Smokeless Coal Company was organized to operate a lease from the N. & W. Railway's subsidiary, the Pocahontas Land Company, with myself as president. This mine produced about 600 tons per day.

At the end of 1922, the Gulf Smokeless Coal Company absorbed the Gulf Coal Company, Wyoming Coal Company, and Covel Smokeless Coal Company, by exchanging stock of Gulf Smokeless for stock of the other three companies. Thereafter all four were operated as the Gulf Smokeless Coal Company.

The years 1920 to 1929 inclusive were good years in the coal business in Southern West Virginia, due largely to repeated strikes in the unionized Northern coal fields and in Great Britain. During all that period wages in our coal fields were higher than in the unionized fields, and attempts by the UMWA to organize Southern West Virginia were unsuccessful. When the depression of 1929 started, certain operators in our field began to cut wages and selling prices in an effort to get a larger share of the reduced market. The Pocahontas field, with a close-knit Operators Association, held wages up for some time. However, in the Winding Gulf field only companies like Slab Fork Coal Company, MacAlpin Coal Company, E. E. White Coal and Gulf Smokeless Coal Company held wages up, while others in the field cut wages. The above companies never went below $4.80 for an eight hour day, while some of their neighbors went to $2.80 for a ten hour day. Consequently, when Roosevelt took office and announced that he would like to see all industry unionized, the Southern West Virginia mines were ripe for organization, and in the fall of 1933 a contract was made with the UMWA. The Gulf Smokeless Coal Company employees were not under this contract until 1934, since until then the union did not secure a majority of the employees. The experience of 1929-1933 had shown that some method of preventing wage cutting was necessary, and the union contract appeared to be the only dependable device to secure this end.

In 1935 the Guffey Bill to regulate sales prices under Federal control was passed. This bill divided the coal industry into two camps. Most of the northern operators and some southern operators (including our company) supported the Bill, while most large southern operators opposed it. They reasoned that they could cut prices, put their competitors out of business, and themselves survive the battle. The Bill was passed and was sustained by the Federal Appellate Court, but was declared unconstitutional by the Supreme Court. This decision was harmful to our coal field, since our freight rates to all major markets in the United States were higher than our competitors, due to our geographical location. This, combined with a recession in business that year (1937), put the coal industry in a bad position.

The start of World War II in 1939 helped the coal business, due to the Lend Lease policy and the re-arming of our own country. When we finally got into the war, the coal business boomed, but under Federal control as to prices, wages and markets. After the war and removal of controls, there was a short boom in demand and prices, due to the strong market for consumer goods.

During the period 1933-1946, the UMWA had demanded and obtained increases in wages from $4 to $5 in 1933 to $16 in 1946. These wages are now (1963) on a basic scale of $24.25, for eight hours underground. Of these 1½ hours are spent in getting to the working place and returning and ½ hour for lunch, leaving 6 hours of actual work.

In 1939 the Hotcoal mine was worked out. In 1937 the Covel mine was shut down and the lease given up by mutual consent between our company and the land owners. By 1941 the Beckley seam was nearly exhausted at the Tams mine. Therefore the lower seam (Pocahontas No. 4), a three foot seam, was opened and brought to 1800-2000 tons per day.

In 1948 we sub-leased our Wyco mine at a good price. In 1955 we decided to take advantage of the good market of the moment and dispose of our company. In order to make the proposition more important and attractive as to tonnage, we bought the property of MacAlpin Coal Company and the stock of Winding Gulf Collieries Company. The MacAlpin mine was in fair condition but had little un-mined tonnage remaining. Winding Gulf Collieries had a very good remaining tonnage but was in very bad condition inside, due to the owners not having been willing to spend the money necessary to put the property in proper shape.

The present owners (Winding Gulf Coals, Inc.) in 1955 asked for an option on the stock of the Gulf Smokeless Coal Company at a satisfactory price—which option was granted. In the fall of 1955 the option was taken up, the stock paid for, and the Gulf Smokeless Coal Company, after 47 years, passed out of existence.

During the life of the Gulf Smokeless Coal Company the writer was president (from 1912), acted as chief engineer and conducted the sales policy of the company. The mine layout and the design of every structure on the property was made by the writer. Every sales contract was made by me. It is a great satisfaction to record that, while paying as high or higher wages and salaries as any competing coal company, we paid a dividend to stockholders every year commencing in 1910. This continued even through the 1929-33 depression. On the original investment of $700,-000 in the four companies, the stockholders received $10,047,540 in cash dividends and $6,489,-600 for their stock. The company mined almost exactly thirty million tons of coal.

6

Personalities in the Smokeless Coal Fields

The miner of 1903 would probably not have known what to make of his 1963 counterpart. Much the same thing might be said of the operator. The early operators were a highly individualistic lot, quite different from today's "organization man." Many were men of little formal education; only a handful had any training in engineering. However, all successful operators had great drive, high native intelligence, willingness to assume large risks and an unusual capacity for hard and sustained work.

In many respects, the old time operator **was** the company. He raised the necessary capital, selected the site, and supervised the building of town and tipple. The operator lived at the mine and was completely familiar with all aspects of the operation. The operator was then no remote figure; indeed, many took pride in knowing each of his employees.

For these reasons, the gulf between operators and miners was relatively small in the early days. At the turn of the century nearly all operators were still living on the job. The Kanawha field was close enough to Charleston to enable one or two from that field to have homes in Charleston and spend week-ends there. Justus

Collins moved to Charleston from Loop Creek in 1903, but all other operators in that field lived at the mines when I came to West Virginia. The operating heads of companies began to build themselves fairly comfortable homes at the mines. Some, like W. D. Ord on the N. & W. Railway and John McGuffin on Loop Creek, built elaborate and costly homes at their mines, but continued to live on the job. When they wanted a taste of luxury, they took trips to the big cities—usually Cincinnati and New York—and stayed at the best hotels. The exodus from the mines to the cities by the presidents of coal companies began after World War I. By 1950 Austin Caperton of Slab Fork and myself were, so far as I know, the only presidents of coal companies still living on the job. The resulting lack of personal contact between operators and their employees certainly did much to increase labor-management difficulties.

It should perhaps be mentioned that the old-time operators tended to be extreme individualists. Many of them had fought their way up against tremendous odds. It is probably true that they were not by nature inclined toward cooperative ventures. This individualism was re-inforced by the practice of the railroads of playing one operator off against the other in an effort to obtain the lowest possible price. Needless to say, this practice did not make for the growth of mutual trust on the part of the operators. Thus, the various operators' associations were not as successful as might be imagined. The associations had some success in setting prices, wages, labor policies and the like in good times. However, they had no really effective method of disciplining their members, and some always "broke loose" under the pressure of declining profits.

By and large, the early operators were coal men and coal men only. What money they made was usually re-invested in some aspect of the coal industry. This, of course, made them highly dependent on the vagaries of a most unstable market. It also accounts for the near or complete disappearance of many once substantial fortunes when the bottom fell out of the coal industry during the 1930's.

Coal mining, unlike gold or uranium mining, does not usually produce the "get-rich-quick" speculator. Substantial fortunes were made in coal, but these were acquired over a period of years. Perhaps for this reason, the coal fields did not produce the flamboyant types so common in our western ore mining areas. Conspicuous consumption on the grand scale was relatively rare. For example, the only private railway car in our section was one George and Herbert Jones used for a short while in the early nineteen twenties on the Guyan Branch of the C. & O. Railway. My company's landlord, the Beaver Coal Company's directors, used to pay an annual visit to their lessees' mines in a private car, but discontinued the visits in the depression.

The early operators lived before the days of "public relations". They had little interest in—indeed they often avoided—personal publicity. For this reason, little is known today of even the most important of the early operators. We have books and articles galore about minor political and literary figures, yet it is often difficult to

find even the birth and death dates of men of
vastly greater importance to the history of West
Virginia. Thus, as a service to future historians,
it seems useful to record here what I can remember of the careers and personalities of the great
figures of the Smokeless Coal Fields. The University Library has been kind enough to check
and supply some dates and details. The men covered are listed alphabetically.

-•-

EDWARD J. BERWIND
(1848-1936)

Fifty years ago Berwind was the "biggest"
name in bituminous coal mining. Berwind was
born into a Philadelphia family of considerable
means. As a relatively young man he acquired a
tract of approximately 30,000 acres of smokeless
coal in Central Pennsylvania and, under the corporate name of Berwind White Coal Mining Company, became a large producer and a power on
the Pennsylvania Railway. He practically mo-
nopolized the ship bunkering business in New
York harbor. This, in the days of coal burning
ships, was of tremendous tonnage. He also controlled the large tonnage power plant business in
New York harbor and had bunker stations in
Cuba and other Caribbean islands.

Beginning to feel the competition of the
New River and Pocahontas fields in New York
and New England, Berwind influenced J. P. Morgan and the Pennsylvania Railway to purchase
control of the Chesapeake and Ohio Railway and
the Norfolk and Western Railway in order to
advance their freight rates to Tidewater. When
this was not entirely effective, Berwind fell back

on the political maxim "if you can't lick them join them" and decided to get into the coal mining business in the New River and Pocahontas fields. W. P. Rend, of Illinois, had opened mines on the Thurmond land on Arbuckle Creek near Thurmond and was shipping a large tonnage. In 1904, Berwind bought this property for approximately $1,000,000. Old timers may still remember "Paddy" Rend exhibiting the check in the Dunglen Hotel bar and buying drinks for all comers. Berwind also bought the properties of the old pioneer, Joe Beury, and in the Norfolk and Western Railway field bought a very large tract on Dry Fork.

Berwind always refused to operate on leased property and would mine coal only on property owned by himself. He would never join any operators association, holding that they were all right for the ordinary operator but were beneath his dignity. When the United States entered World War I, coal suddenly rose to $5.00 per ton, from the $1.70 price of 1916. An Illinois operator, Francis Peabody, was a friend of Wilson's Secretary of the Interior, Lane, and at Lane's suggestion called a meeting of eighteen operators (of whom the writer was one) in Washington in April, 1917. Mr. Berwind, looking as if he was somewhat ashamed of his company, asked the writer, sitting beside him, "What are the names of these people?" A price of $3.50 was agreed to by the meeting, but it was repudiated by Josephus Daniels, the Secretary of the Navy. Wilson's Fuel Administration later fixed the price at $2.70. It was the first and last time Berwind attended a coal operators meeting. Incidentally, this meeting was the beginning of the National Coal Association.

A scene typical of Berwind occurred in 1928, when the writer and Isaac T. Mann were trying to consolidate the Smokeless Fields of West Virginia. After lunching at the Recess Club in New York, we were walking towards the entrance, when we passed Berwind's table. He stopped us and said he had heard of our effort and thought it an excellent thing. Mr. Mann said, "Mr. Berwind will you join us?" Berwind, with a horrified look as if we had committed "lese majeste", answered "Good God, no. I couldn't get mixed up in such a group."

Today the Berwind empire has shrunk, and the company is of no great importance in the industry. "Sic transit gloria mundi".

—•—

JOSEPH L. BEURY
(1842-1903)

Beury was a native of Schuylkill County, Pennsylvania. After the Civil War he became a mine superintendent in the Pennsylvania fields. In that capacity, he became engaged in a bitter struggle with the Molly McGuires, a secret group of terrorists. His employers finally decided that they would have to send him from the area in order to protect his life. Thus, in 1872 Beury came to Fayette County, West Virginia and located on Laurel Creek at Quinnimont. He began mining there and the next year started to ship coal over the newly completed C. & O. Beury was a member of the first coal company organized in Fayette (New River Coal Co.). In 1876 Beury, along with Jenkin Jones and others, developed what are

now known as the Fire Creek Mines. In 1884,
Beury, with his brother and John Cooper, formed
the Mill Creek Coal and Coke Company—the first
lease in the Flat Top Coal Field.

Beury is generally regarded as the pioneer
operator in the New River Field. He came to the
area when it was practically a wilderness. Beury
began with little money or technical training. Indeed, legend has it that he and Cooper started
what became the Caperton Mine with one mule
and a borrowed harness. However, Beury had
keen native intelligence, courage and great energy. His position was recognized by Governor
Atkinson, who appointed him a colonel on his
staff. However, he continued to be known as
"Captain Joe."

JONATHAN P. BOWEN
(1830-1902)

Like many of the early operators, Bowen
was born in Wales and brought up in the Pennsylvania coal fields (Schuylkill County). He was
both able and ambitious and became superintendent of mines in Pennsylvania and south-west-
ern Virginia. In 1884 Bowen and William Booth
opened one of the early mines—generally regarded as the fourth—in the Flat-Top Field. Located at Freeman, Mercer County, the organization was first called William Booth and Co. However, in 1889 the name was changed to the Booth-
Bowen Coal and Coke Company. Bowen succeeded
Booth as president and continued in that position
until his death. He was succeeded in that office
by his son William H. (generally known as Harry).

GEORGE HENRY CAPERTON
(1860-1928)

Caperton was born in Lynchburg and educated at Virginia Polytechnic Institute. He came to West Virginia in 1880 and became a mine superintendent in the Fire Creek, Fayette County, area. In 1907, George (always known as "Harry") and W. Gaston Caperton secured a lease from the Beaver Coal Corp. on the Virginian main line and opened the first smokeless coal mine on the Virginian Railway at Slab Fork. Caperton was at various times president of the Slab Fork Coal Company, the Scotia Coal and Coke Company and the New River Coal Company, a sales company formed in 1912.

W. GASTON CAPERTON
(1869-1945)

Younger brother of George H. A graduate engineer (Lafayette College), W. G. Caperton followed his brother to the West Virginia coal fields in 1894. He worked first as an engineer and then (1900) became superintendent of the Wright Colliery Company on Piney Creek. He and his brother worked both closely and well together, and Gaston became president of Slab Fork after Harry's death in 1928. The Slab Fork mine is now operated by Gaston's son and grandson, both named Austin.

JUSTUS COLLINS
(1857-1934)

Collins was born in Clayton, Alabama. While Collins had little formal education, he was endowed with high intelligence and great ambition. By the time he was thirty, he had become an official of the Woodward Iron Company of Birmingham. In 1887 Collins moved to Goodwill, in Mercer County, West Virginia. Here he became superintendent of several mines. With the financial backing of James and R. T. Watts of Lynchburg, he opened the Collins Colliery Company at Glen Jean in 1893. Later he opened the Whipple mine on a branch of Loop Creek. In 1906 he sold both the Collins and Whipple mines to the New River Company and formed the Superior Pocahontas Coal Co. In 1910 he opened the Winding Gulf mine on the Virginian Rail Road. In 1929 Collins consolidated his holdings under the name of Winding Gulf Colleries. The principal companies involved were the Louisville Coal and Coke Company (Goodwill), the Winding Gulf Colliery Company, and the Superior Pocahontas Coal Company. The Smokeless Fuel Company was established as the sales agency.

JOHN COOPER
(1842-1899)

Cooper was born in England and went to work in the mines at the age of six. He came to the Pennsylvania coal fields in 1862 and moved to West Virginia eleven years later. He is known to have worked in mining operations at Quinnimont and Hawks Nest. In 1884 he, along with J. L. Beury, opened the Mill Creek mine—generally regarded as the first operation in the Flat-Top Field. The Mill Creek Coal & Coke Co. (incorporated in 1890) soon became a highly profitable enterprise. The village of Coopers (Mercer County) is named after John Cooper. Cooper was followed in the coal business by his sons Thomas

(1869-1911) and Edward (1873-1928). Edward was also a Member of Congress from 1914 to 1918.

—

SAMUEL L. DIXON
(1856-1934)

Born in England, Dixon came to Fayette County in 1877. At first he worked for an uncle, Fred Faulkner. He then became an assistant to Symington Macdonald, the general manager of the Great Kanawha Colliery Company. In 1893, with Macdonald and C. G. Blake of Cincinnati, he opened the Macdonald mine on Loop Creek, and later the Sugar Creek, Scarbro, Carlisle, Oakwood, Stuart, Parral and Wingrove mines. In 1904, he interested P. W. Sprague of Boston and several other New England business men in joining him in the coal business. The next year they organized the New River Company, with Dixon as president and general manager. The company then owned the Price Hill (on land purchased by Dixon in 1899), Sherwood, Sprague, Skelton, Cranberry and Prosperity mines. In 1906 it purchased from McGuffin the Harvey, Dunloop and Prudence mines, thus becoming the largest producer in the New River Field.

Dixon was also active in the building of railroads. In 1903 he built (under the corporate name of the White Oak Railway Company) an extension of the C. & O. through Oak Hill to the Stuart Mine. When the Virginian Railway was built, the White Oak Railway constructed a two mile branch line from Oak Hill to connect with the Virginian at Bishop. The Piney River and Paint Creek Rail-

road—running through Beckley to Cranberry—
was built by Dixon in 1906.

In 1912 Dixon resigned as president of the
New River Company. There had been a brief
boom in the coal market in 1905-06, when the
New River Company had just been formed. The
New England directors urged Dixon to buy up
operating mines and to begin the development of
coal lands in order to increase production. These
purchases (Harvey, Dunloop, Prudence, Beckley
Slope, Mabscot) called for one third down payment in 1906, and one third each year in 1907 and
1908. When the "Bankers Panic" of 1907-08 occurred, the New River Company was faced with
completing purchase payments and the development of coal lands. However, money was tight,
and the price of coal dropped from $1.30 to 90
cents. The directors threw the blame on Dixon
for their own misjudgment, and by 1912 relations were so strained that his resignation became inevitable. Dixon and two associates owned
the land at the Price Hill mine, and when the new
management of the New River Company stopped
operation at Price Hill in order to force a change
in the lease terms, Dixon took back the property,
persuaded Sprague to put up the necessary money
and resumed operation at Price Hill (1913). As
World War I began the next year, the operation
was financially successful for a number of years.

Dixon was a man of tremendous energy and
drive, with a very quick and keen mind. His interests were not confined to coal. He was at various times owner of several papers in Raleigh
and Fayette counties. He was also the Republican
political boss of Fayette County and for years

dominated politics in the county. Tales of "King Samuel" and his political adventures have become part of the folklore of the area.

—•—

J. FRED EFFINGER
(1846-1932)

Effinger, as a young Staunton, Virginia lawyer, was appointed administrator of an estate which included coal land on New River. In this way, he got into coal mining. In 1887, Effinger, with the writer's father, Ferdinand Howald, and two others, organized the Rush Run Coal Company. They opened the Rush Run mine (about two miles west of Thurmond) with a capital of $20,000. This illustrates with what a modest amount of money a mine could then be opened. Later he opened several other adjacent mines, finally consolidating seven mines, with himself as president, Howald as general manager and John Laing as general superintendent. In 1900 Effinger organized the Wright Coal & Coke Company, with W. G. Caperton as general manager. He was also elected president of the New River Consolidated Coal Company, which included nearly all New River producers, and which was organized in an effort to exercise some control over the price of their coal. He knew little of practical coal mining but was a shrewd and financially successful business man. As a classmate and fraternity brother at the University of Virginia of W. C. Bullitt, he was able to secure for the writer the lease of the Tams mine, since Bullitt was then the president of the Beaver Coal Company.

JAMES D. FRANCIS
(1884-1958)

The producer of the largest annual coal tonnage in the state is the Island Creek Coal Company, which started with approximately 35,000 acres of land on the Island Creek branch of the Guyandotte River. This land was in the area where "Devil Anse" Hatfield, the patriarch of the Hatfield clan, lived. This company now controls considerably over 200,000 acres of coal land, containing both high and low volatile coals, operating on the C. & O. Railway and the N. & W. Railway. Connected with the company from its formation was James D. Francis, a native of Kentucky. Starting as land agent, he was successively legal adviser, vice-president, president, and chairman of the board. He directed the policy of the company by advice or executive control for nearly fifty years. A man of tireless energy, he worked an eighteen hour day in the company's interest. His company pioneered in the Logan Field the building of attractive houses in well planned mining towns. While operating on a non-union basis, his company paid the highest wages. When, in 1933, President Roosevelt pressured the change to a unionized basis, Francis was one of a committee of four appointed by the coal operators to negotiate, under N. I. R. A., a union contract. He was a director of every association affecting the coal mining industry and also a director of the U. S. Chamber of Commerce. A very religious man, he was the largest contributor to the Presbyterian Church in Huntington, where he lived. There is no doubt that he was one of the

most influential figures in coal mining in West
Virginia.

—•—

JOHN FREEMAN
(1822-1892)

Freeman was born in England, but moved to
the coal fields of Pennsylvania about 1850. In
1884 he and Jenkin Jones opened the Simmons
Creek Mine (for an account of this venture see
under Jenkin Jones). The village of Freeman in
Mercer County is named after this early and successful coal operator. Freeman was followed in
the coal business by his sons Charles W. (1873-
1930) and W. G. Freeman.

—•—

THE JONES FAMILY

The Jones family came from Amherst County, Virginia, in the early 19th century to Fayette
County. They developed the Lundale farm at Oak
Hill, a property still owned by the family. When
Loop Creek was opened in 1893, Charles T. Jones
(1849-1911) and his brother George W. Jones
(1857-1937) opened a mine at Red Star on their
own property. Running into a "fault" at the out-
set, they barely survived financially the unex-
pected expense of driving through 300 feet of
rock. George Jones himself worked as a member
of the rock drilling crew. Besides operating Red
Star, the Jones family leased coal land to the New
River Company at Scarbro, and to McGuffin at
Prudence. C. T. Jones' sons, George and Herbert,
opened large mines at Amherst and Lundale on
the Guyandotte River, and Herbert Jones' sons
are now operating these mines. This family has
therefore for three generations, with great fi-

nancial success, mined coal in Southern West Virginia. Theirs is one of the relatively few instances of a family already living on the land, which has continuously and successfully carried on coal operations.

--◆--

JAMES ELWOOD JONES
(1872-1932)

James E. was the son of Jenkin Jones. After graduation from the Columbia University School of Mines, he followed his father in the coal business and became vice president and general manager of the Pocahontas Fuel Company. Jones was an engineer of unusual ability. He invented and developed a number of machines for the loading and handling of coal and slate. Jones was also very active in civic affairs in McDowell County and served for some twenty-four years on the County Court. Without it being generally known, he sent at least fifty boys to school or college at his own expense. Jones won the Republican nomination for United States Senate in 1930 but was badly defeated by M. M. Neely in the general election.

--◆--

JENKIN JONES
(1841-1916)

Born in Wales, Jones went to work in the mines as a boy. He came to the United States in 1863 and worked in the Pennsylvania fields. Jones came to West Virginia in the 1870's and worked at Quinnimont and Fire Creek. He and J. L. Beury were pioneers in that area. In 1884 Jones and John Freeman acquired a lease from the Flat-Top Coal Land Association and opened the Simmons Creek mine, near the present site

of Bramwell. Like most early operators, Jones
and Freeman started with little more than de-
termination. It was said that their capital equipment consisted of one mule, one mine car and a
few picks and shovels. Both men dug coal themselves. In 1889 the partners formed the Caswell
Creek Coal and Coke Company, and gradually ex-
panded their operations. In 1907 the Caswell Creek
Coal and Coke Company was incorporated into the
newly-formed Pocahontas Fuel Company.

--◆--

JAMES LAING
(1847-1907)

Laing was born in Lanarkshire, Scotland
and emigrated to the Pennsylvania coal fields in
1867. In 1878 he came to Fayette County, West
Virginia. Ten years later he moved to Raleigh
County to become an official of the Royal Coal
and Coke Company. In 1896 Laing opened a mine
on the C. & O. Railroad at Sun, on Loop Creek
(The Sun Coal and Coke Company). James Laing
was the uncle of John Laing and the father of
John B., both of whom were important figures in
the coal industry.

--◆--

JOHN LAING
(1865-1943)

Laing was born in Lanarkshire, Scotland,
and came to Fayette County in 1884. John Laing's
uncle, James Laing, opened the Royal mine at
Prince and later opened Sun mine on Loop Creek,
one of the largest producers in the New River
field. John Laing dug coal in Pennsylvania,
Ohio, the Kanawha Field, and finally went
to work at Rush Run where he became succes-

sively boss driver, foreman, superintendent, and finally general superintendent of the group of seven mines of which J. F. Effinger was president and Ferdinand Howald general manager. When these mines were sold to C. J. Wittenberg, president of the C. & O. Coal Agency, in 1906, John Laing opened the MacAlpin mine on the Winding Gulf and also became interested in mines in Logan County and on Cabin Creek*. In 1908 he was appointed Chief of the Mine Department of West Virginia and served through September, 1913. He also headed the Wyatt Coal Sales Company. Laing was a typical example of the American self made man, starting at the bottom and working his way to the top by energy and intelligence. His uncle, James Laing, and the latter's son, John B. Laing, after the 1906 sale, invested in coal land in Greenbrier County.

WILLIAM LECKIE
(1857-1920)

Leckie was born in Scotland and went to work in the mines as a boy. At the age of twenty-one he came to Schuylkill County, Pennsylvania. There he worked in the mines and managed to save enough money to become a student at Dickinson Seminary. From 1882 to 1901 he enjoyed an increasingly successful career with several Pennsylvania coal companies. In 1901 he came to the Pocahontas field as superintendent of the

---

*Wittenberg opened two mines, called "Wittenberg I & II," now called Eccles. The mines were operated with varying fortune until 1923. At that time W. P. Tams, Jr., acting at the request of the owners, negotiated a sale of the property to Daniel Wentz, head of the Stonega Coal Company, of Big Stone Gap, Virginia.

Pocahontas Collieries Company. In 1907 he entered business for himself and became extremely successful. He was president of such companies as West Virginia Pocahontas Coal, Lathrop Coal, Panther Coal and Douglas Coal. At operators' meetings it was amusing to hear Leckie and John Laing get into arguments and lapse into their native "braid Scots" in their excitement.

JOHN J. LINCOLN
(1865-1948)

Lincoln was born in Lancaster County, Pennsylvania and educated at Lehigh University. He was graduated from that institution in 1889 with a degree in civil engineering. Lincoln was employed for several years with the United States Coast and Geodetic Survey. However, in 1893 he moved to the newly-opened coal fields in McDowell County. Here he was highly successful and became general manager of the Crozer Coal and Land Company, vice president of the Page Coal and Coke Company, and an officer or director of a number of other coal and land companies. Lincoln was the founder and first secretary of the Pocahontas Operators Association. He was an extremely polite and affable man in personal intercourse—a somewhat rare quality in coal operators of that era.

THOMAS GAYLORD McKELL
(1845-1904)

Thomas G. McKell was a native of Chillicothe, Ohio. He acquired in 1870 a 12,500 acre tract on Loop Creek. This was a wedding present to his wife, Jean, from her father, John Dun. Mc-

Kell increased this tract to approximately 25,000 acres by purchasing adjacent land from Morris Harvey, Samuel Coit and others. His holdings were underlaid by the great Sewell and Fire Creek seams. McKell persuaded M. E. Ingalls, president of the C. & O., to construct a branch to his property—promising to deed a right-of-way for the line. (It is said that McKell and Ingalls later fell out, and McKell restricted the right-of-way to the ends of the cross-ties.) The line was completed in 1893, and the first car of coal was shipped from the Collins Colliery Company at Glen Jean in November of that year.

At first, McKell confined himself to leasing his land. However, in 1900 he organized the McKell Coal and Coke Company in order to develop some of the property himself. Among the mines he opened were those at Kilsyth, Oswald, Graham and Tamroy. In 1896 McKell built the opera house at Glen Jean and five years later the Dunglen Hotel at Thurmond. It was a fine (for those days) hotel, with an excellent dining room which the young people of the area used for dances. The hotel was destroyed by fire on July 22, 1930.

—

WILLIAM McKELL
(1871-1939)

Son of Thomas G. After graduation from Yale (1893), he became associated with his father in the coal business and assumed general management of the business after the elder McKell's death. He was also a banker and in 1909 organized the Bank of Glen Jean. William McKell, a very wealthy man, was extremely quiet and self-effacing but very determined. He was the first man to obtain a court decision for damages against the UMWA—it is said for $500,000. William McKell was a bachelor, and after his death in 1939, his coal property was sold by the executors to the New River Company.

McQUAIL FAMILY

The first representative of the family in the Smokeless Fields was William H. (1845-1913). He opened the Ennis mine in 1888, shortly after the extension of the Norfolk & Western Rail Road up Flipping Creek. McQuail was known as the "Duke of Venice" (a play on the name of the mine), and was a most colorful person. It was said that on pay day night he required his salaried men to play poker with him, and that by morning he had recovered their salaries. Be that as it may, he was a most successful operator. He was shrewd enough to make a long-term sales agreement with the Seaboard Air Line Railroad. The Railroad furnished him enough coal cars to run six days a week. At the time, his competitors could get Norfolk & Western cars for only four days a week. McQuail's organization was called Turkey Gap Coal and Coke Co., with headquarters at Dot, West Virginia. His son, Edward J. McQuail (1873-1924), succeeded him in the business. The family disposed of their coal property quite recently.

ISAAC T. MANN
(1863-1932)

Mann was born in Greenbrier County and became associated with the Greenbrier Valley Bank. However, he recognized the opportunities

in the coal fields and in 1889 joined the Bank of
Bramwell, of which he soon became president.
The Bank of Bramwell became fabulously successful under Mann's direction. The Bank reached
its zenith in 1923, when it had assets of over
13 million—perhaps the richest small-town bank
in the nation. (It merged with the First National
Bank of Bluefield in 1933.)

As a banker, Mann had opportunities to in-
vest in the Pocahontas mines, and formed a group
of them into the Pocahontas Consolidated Coal
Company with himself as president. In 1910 he
formed the Pocahontas Fuel Company to sell the
product of the mines. This large tonnage defect-
ing from the firm of Castner, Curran, and Bullitt started the break-up of this agency's monopoly
of sales in the Pocahontas field—and Bullitt's
death finished it. Other mines and groups of mines
followed suit and established their own agencies
or went to other agencies. Mann became very
wealthy, and in 1913 tried to get elected by the
Legislature to the United States Senate. William
S. Edwards and Davis Elkins entered the race
and the battle grew so bitter that the politicians
finally got them all to withdraw. Mann later
moved to Washington where he died in 1932, after financial reverses in the depression.

—•—

ERSKINE MILLER
(1846-1897)

Miller, of Staunton, Virginia, operated a
wholesale provision business. Through indebted-
ness of the mine, he became owner of Fire Creek,
one of the oldest mines on the Chesapeake and
Ohio Railway. His engineer was a young German,

Ferdinand Howald, afterward manager of Rush Run, Red Ash, and other mines; and his mine foreman was Jenkin Jones, a Welsh miner who later went over to the Pocahontas Field and became one of the wealthiest of the operators in that region. Mr. Miller was a successful operator in a modest way, but was perhaps better known as an early employer of men who later became figures of great importance.

—•—

PATTERSON FAMILY

Stephen J. Patterson was a native of Dayton, Ohio and a brother of John H. Patterson, founder of the National Cash Register Company. He founded the Weyanoke Coal and Coke Company on the Norfolk & Western Railroad. In 1910 Patterson opened the Hotcoal mine on the Winding Gulf Branch of the Virginian. Two years later the writer and his associates purchased this mine from Patterson. Patterson's son, Robert D., inherited and operated his father's holdings. He was the first operator who offered prizes for the best kept yards and gardens in his town, with the result that anyone passing the Weyanoke mine was struck with the neatness and cleanliness of the place. The writer followed the example of his good friend Bob Patterson in this respect and with the same excellent results. R. D. Patterson died in 1944, and his executors sold the family coal properties.

—•—

W. J. RICHARDS
(1868-1949)

Richards, of Welsh descent, became head of one of the large anthracite companies in Pennsylvania. He was an investor in Norfolk and Western mines and also in the Pemberton Coal & Coke Company on the Winding Gulf Branch of the Virginian, with mines at Pemberton and Big Stick. After World War I, his son W. A. (Al) Richards (1896-1940), on his return from military service, became operating head of both the Norfolk and Western Railway and the Virginian Railway mines of the company. Young Richards was a man of the greatest energy, a graduate of Lehigh University (where he was on the football team) and most active in all operator association work. He was also very active in promoting the Guffey Bill and the District Board created by the bill. His death some twenty-three years ago was a distinct loss to the coal fraternity.

W. D. THURMOND
(1820-1910)

Thurmond came to Fayette County about 1842 from Amherst County, Virginia. Thurmond acquired a considerable acreage of coal land in what was to become the heart of the New River coal field. He was not himself an operator, but leased his land to W. P. Rend and, later, to the Berwind-White interests. Thurmond's son (Joseph S.) and grandson (Walter R.) became prominent figures in the coal industry. Walter R. Thurmond, after working as an engineer for Samuel Dixon, opened mines in Logan County and at one time operated four successful properties. He was president of the Logan Coal Operators Association and was very active in the 1920 fight against the UMWA. After selling out in the depression, he became District Director of Internal Revenue at Parkersburg and later Secretary of the Southern Coal Operators Association.

—•—

JOHN J. TIERNEY
(1857-1923)

Born in Schuylkill County, Pennsylvania, Tierney was trained as an engineer and had considerable experience in the Pennsylvania coal fields. In 1885 he became chief engineer of the Bluestone Coal & Coke Company. Three years later he accepted a position as chief engineer for the Crozer Land Company and president of the Powhatan Coal & Coke Company. In 1895 he became president of the Pocahontas Company, a sales and marketing concern. He was one of the organizers of the National Coal Association and was its treasurer until his death. When the Smokeless Coal Operators Association was formed, he was elected president and remained as such until his death.

—•—

LAURENCE E. TIERNEY
(1860-1922)

Brother of John J., Col. Laurence E. Tierney was born in Schuylkill County, Pennsylvania and graduated in 1882 from Villanova College. He then took post-graduate work at Georgetown University. In 1886 he became assistant mining engineer for the Flat-Top Land Trust. Three years later he became general manager of the Powhatan Coal & Coke Co. In the following years he became an officer of a number of other coal companies—Lynchburg Coal & Coke (1891), Eureka Coal & Coke (1892), Elk Ridge Coal & Coke (1893) etc. In 1907 he formed the Tierney Land

Company, which included substantial holdings in Pike County, Kentucky. The Tierney Mining Company operated there until its sale during World War II. Tierney was an important figure in the Democratic Party in the area. He was a delegate to the Democratic National Convention in 1912 and served as an advisor to President Wilson on the coal industry. His colonelcy was by way of appointment to the military staff of Governor MacCorkle.

His sons, Laurence E. Jr. and Lewis (now deceased), succeeded him. Laurence E. Tierney, Jr. is treasurer of the Southern Coal Producers Association and of the Operators Association of the Williamson Fields and is a director of both. He is also a director of the National Coal Association, the National Coal Policy Conference, and the American Mining Congress. He is also president and a director of the West Virginia Coal Association.

—•—

E. E. WHITE
(1858-1930)

White was born in England and came to America with his family at the age of 10. His father worked in the anthracite mines of Pennsylvania, where White started as a trapper boy. After finishing public school he became a school teacher. When the great anthracite strike occurred in 1902, White secured the right to mine coal from the outcroppings of a large mine, and as the striking miners and their families needed coal, they permitted White to operate. Although producing only a small tonnage, the price of anthracite had risen so high that White was able to make considerable money. With this money, and with his father-in-law, Bickle, as superintendent, White came to West Virginia and obtained a lease from the Beaver Coal Company. In 1904 he opened the Beckley mine near the town of Beckley. In 1906 he sold this mine to the New River Coal Company at a good profit and then obtained another lease from the Beaver Coal Company, on which he opened Glen White and Stotesbury mines in 1909 and 1910. In 1925 he sold these profitable mines at a good price and retired to Mt. Carmel, Pennsylvania, where he died a few years later. White was one of the first operators in the Winding Gulf field and was the first president of the Winding Gulf Operators Association (1908). He continued in that office until he sold out. White was a shrewd business man, without great technical knowledge, but a man of fine character.

7

Place Names in the Smokeless Coal Fields

Visitors to the Smokeless Coal Fields often comment on the—to them—strange names of the coal camps. Within a relatively few miles one finds villages bearing what appear to be English, Scotch and Mexican names. Other villages seem to bear family names, while the origin of other names may appear totally incomprehensible.

The principal explanation for the haphazard and often puzzling choice of place names was doubtless the rapid growth of the area. The Winding Gulf, for example, was a wilderness in 1908; a decade later several dozen coal camps had been built. Obviously, these had to be named and named quickly. Their builders had neither the time nor the inclination to worry greatly about the most appropriate choices.

The operator who constructed the coal camp usually supplied the name. There was then no question of consulting historical societies or holding popular referendums. Indeed, the camp was often named before its residents arrived. In any case, the operator was usually free to call his village almost anything he chose—subject only to the approval of the postal authorities. If he wished to name it after a mine he had visited in Mexico, there was nothing to prevent him from doing so.

Several characteristics of the place names in this area are immediately apparent. One is the large number of villages bearing English and Scotch names. These, of course, reflect the national origins of many of the early operators. Samuel Dixon, for example, was especially fond of giving English names to his mines. Another indication of national origins is the widespread use of the Scotch word "glen." This was often combined with a personal or family name in naming a village—Glen Jean, Glen White etc.

Listed below in alphabetical order are some of the more interesting proper names in the Smokeless Coal area, together with suggestions as to their origins.

BERWIND (McDowell County). Named for Edward J. Berwind. (See page 77 for biographical sketch)

BRAMWELL (Mercer County). Named for J. H. Bramwell, an engineer who came with Captain Welch's party to investigate the coal resources of the area. He later became general manager of the Crozer Land Company.

CARLISLE (Fayette County). Named by Samuel Dixon after the city in England.

COOPERS (Mercer County). Named after John Cooper. (See page 82 for biographical sketch)

DUHRING (Mercer County). Named after C. H. Duhring, local manager of the Flat Top Coal Land enterprises until his death in 1891.

ECKMAN (McDowell County). Named for John W. Eckman, for many years general manager of the Pulaski Iron Company.

ENNIS (McDowell County). Maiden name of Mrs. William McQuail, wife of the original operator.

EPPERLY (Raleigh County). Named for Lamar Epperly, official of several mining companies.

FIRECO (Raleigh County). Any name indicating heat was thought to have advertising value. Thus the use of such names as Fireco and Hotcoal.

FREEMAN (Mercer County). Named for John Freeman. (See page 87 for biographical sketch)

GARY (McDowell County). Named after Elbert H. Gary, Chairman of the U. S. Steel Corporation.

GLEN JEAN (Fayette County). Jean was the name of the wife of Thomas G. McKell, the landowner. (See page 91 for biographical sketch)

GLEN WHITE (Raleigh County). Named after E. E. White. (See page 98 for biographical sketch)

HELEN (Raleigh County). Named after the daughter of President G. W. Stevens of the C. & O. Railway.

HERNDON (Wyoming County). Probably named after A. M. Herndon, an official of the Winding Gulf Colliery Company and other concerns.

ITMANN (Wyoming County). Named in honor of Isaac T. Mann. (See page 93 for biographical sketch)

JENKINJONES (McDowell County). Named after Jenkin Jones, pioneer operator. (See page 88 for biographical sketch)

KEYSTONE (McDowell County). Named after the "Keystone State." Many of the developers of the area came from Pennsylvania.

KIMBALL (McDowell County). Named in honor of Frederick J. Kimball, president of the Norfolk and Western Railway.

LANARK (Raleigh County). Named by James K. Laing for his home county in Scotland.

LECKIE (McDowell County). Named after William Leckie, pioneer operator. (See page 90 for biographical sketch)

LOCHGELLY (Fayette County). Before the great mine explosion of January 29, 1907 and for a short time thereafter, the town was known as Stuart. This name was given by Mr. Dixon, after a relative. The change of name was made by the succeeding management in an effort to help people forget the disaster.

McALPIN (Raleigh County). Named by John Laing in honor of his mother, whose maiden name was McAlpin.

McDONALD (Fayette County). Named after Symington McDonald, pioneer operator.

MABEN (Wyoming County). Named after J. C. Maben of Philadelphia, who with Major Jed Hotchkiss, purchased the 90,000 acre James Welch patent.

MABSCOTT (Raleigh County). A combination of the names of the town's first coal operator

(Cyrus H. Scott) and his fiancee (Mable Shinn)

MAITLAND (McDowell County). Maiden name of the wife of Howard H. Houston, of the Houston Coal and Coke Company.

MATOAKA (Mercer County). Another name for Pocahontas. The fact that the Pocahontas Mine was the first extremely successful mine in this area led to the use of Indian names for other mines. Weyanoke, Winona and Shawnee are examples.

MAYBEURY (McDowell County). Named for two of the early coal operators, Col. A. J. May and William Beury.

MEAD (Raleigh County). Named for C. H. Mead, a coal operator.

NORTHFORK (McDowell County). Named from its location at the junction of the north and south forks of Elkhorn River.

PAGE (Fayette County). Named for Capt. William N. Page, pioneer coal operator.

PARRAL (Fayette County). Named after a mine in Mexico which Samuel Dixon had visited.

QUINNIMONT (Fayette County). From the Latin—"five mountains."

RHODELL (Raleigh County). Named for I. J. Rhodes, one of the founders. An earlier name was Rhodesdale.

SCARBRO (Fayette County). Named by Samuel Dixon after the English town of Scarborough. The Post Office required the shortened form.

SKELTON (Raleigh County). Another example of Mr. Dixon's use of the names of English towns. It was his birthplace.

SLAB FORK (Raleigh County). Named after the creek near which the village is located.

SOPHIA (Raleigh County). Named for Sophia McGinnis, wife of an early settler.

SPRAGUE (Raleigh County) Named after P. W. Sprague, the head of C. H. Sprague Co.

STONE COAL (Raleigh County). Stone coal was the name formerly used for coal, to distinguish it from charcoal.

STOTESBURY (Raleigh County). Named by E. E. White in honor of Edward T. Stotesbury, president of the Beaver Coal Company.

THAYER (Fayette County). Probably named for J. G. Thayer, official of several mining companies.

THURMOND (Fayette County). Named for Captain W. D. Thurmond, who acquired the area on which the town is located in 1873 as payment for surveying work.

URY (Raleigh County). Corruption of Uriah, from Uriah Cook, land owner.

VIVIAN (McDowell County). Named for William Vivian, partner in the London banking house of Vivian, Gray & Company. This company had large financial interests in the Norfolk & Western Railway.

WILCOE (McDowell County). A combination of William Coe, an engineer of the Norfolk and

Western Railway while the Tug Fork branch was under construction.

WYCO (Wyoming County). An abbreviation of the Wyoming Coal Company, which began production in this location in 1915.

PRODUCTION OF COAL IN THE SMOKELESS COAL FIELDS OF WEST VIRGINIA

	1890	1900	1910	1920	1930	1947*	1960
Fayette Co.	1,458,638	5,092,642	10,516,327	8,708,012	11,766,334	15,171,500	4,402,741
McDowell Co.	564,729	4,639,154	13,651,904	17,715,824	20,788,333	26,542,937	14,802,004
Mercer Co.	833,731	1,172,569	2,848,011	2,486,440	4,012,569	3,063,842	677,177
Raleigh Co.	——	76,563	2,853,448	7,748,634	14,540,678	15,167,754	7,124,177
Wyoming Co.	——	——	——	1,424,068	2,238,864	6,110,051	10,747,825
Total	2,857,098	10,980,928	29,869,690	38,082,978	53,346,778	66,056,084	37,753,924

*1947 was the year of peak production.